Radical Surrender

LETTERS TO SEMINARIANS

"Father Najim has written a very fine collection of letters in the tradition of *lectio divina*. Seminarians who take the time to prayerfully consider his words will move far along the path of discerning a priestly vocation."

Cardinal Sean O'Malley, OFM, Cap.
Archdiocese of Boston

"In this superb collection of meditative letters, Father Najim provides invaluable spiritual lessons to seminarians, and exemplifies the fatherly attributes a vocation director must possess to guide young men towards the gift of priesthood."

Msgr. Robert Panke, STL
Vocation Director, Archdiocese of Washington, D.C.

Radical Surrender speaks straight to the heart of any seminarian. I only wish I had received such letters when I was in the seminary! It is a must read for all seminarians and for vocation directors. Clearly the fruit of prayer, this book provides encouragement through the ups and downs of seminary life, and an invitation to give all to the Lord.

Father Len Plazewski
President, National Conference of Diocesan Vocation Directors

"At a time when the role of fatherhood is under attack within our culture, Father Najim writes personal letters to seminarians as a spiritual father to his sons. These prayerful, passionate, practical letters direct seminarians to a heartfelt and authentic relationship with Jesus Christ as the core of their priestly formation."

Christina Lynch, PsyD
St. John Vianney Seminary, Denver

Radical Surrender is at once deeply spiritual and eminently practical. These "spiritual letters" will inspire the hearts of seminarians. The book can also serve as a tool to assist the work of seminary formators in spiritual direction or formation advising. *Radical Surrender* is a joy to read; I believe that those who prayerfully receive it will find rest and refreshment in the Heart of Christ.

Father David L. Toups, STD
USCCB Secretariat of Clergy, Consecrated Life and Vocations

"In the tradition of Catherine Doherty, Father Michael Najim has written a most valuable series of "letters to seminarians" which speak eternal truths through clear, contemporary language and images. His own faith, wisdom and warm personality penetrate each page. A must read for all seminarians and vocation directors of the New Evangelization."

Father Bill Kelly, STD
Director, Office for Clergy Support and Ongoing Formation
Adjunct Spiritual Director, St. John's Seminary, Boston

Radical Surrender
LETTERS TO SEMINARIANS

Father Michael Najim

THE INSTITUTE FOR PRIESTLY FORMATION
IPF PUBLICATIONS

NIHIL OBSTAT: Father Timothy J. Reilly, JCL

IMPRIMATUR: † Most Reverend Thomas J. Tobin
                 Bishop of Providence

THE INSTITUTE FOR PRIESTLY FORMATION
IPF PUBLICATIONS
2500 California Plaza
Omaha, Nebraska 68178
www.IPFpublications.com

Printed in the United States of America
ISBN-13: 978-0-9800455-8-1
ISBN-10: 0-9800455-8-4

Cover design by Timothy D. Boatright
Marketing Associates, U.S.A.
Tampa, Florida

The Institute for Priestly Formation
Mission Statement

The Institute for Priestly Formation was founded to assist bishops in the spiritual formation of diocesan seminarians and priests in the Roman Catholic Church. The Institute responds to the need to foster spiritual formation as the integrating and governing principle of all aspects of priestly formation. Inspired by the biblical-evangelical spirituality of Ignatius Loyola, this spiritual formation has as its goal the cultivation of a deep interior communion with Christ; from such communion the priest shares in Christ's own pastoral charity. In carrying out its mission, the Institute directly serves diocesan seminarians and priests as well as those who are responsible for diocesan priestly formation.

The Institute for Priestly Formation
Creighton University
2500 California Plaza
Omaha, Nebraska 68178
www.creighton.edu/ipf
ipf@creighton.edu

Table of Contents

Foreword

My Dear Friends in Christ,

The most important aspects of the discernment process are prayer and spiritual reflection. Through personal communion with Jesus, we come to understand who we are and what we are being called to in this life. Meaningful prayer requires time and focus. We can and should offer many prayers in the midst of our daily activities, but securing a vocation calls for times of spiritual reflection "set apart" from the demands of schedules and commitments. Father Najim envisions these letters to be read as *lectio divina*. Prayerful reading is not a hurried process or an assignment to be completed, but rather an opportunity to proceed along the journey of developing a closer relationship with the Lord and a better understanding of how He is calling you.

Our ability to embrace God's will with trust presupposes that we know God and His love. If we really know that God is all-loving and at the same time all-powerful, we will not be afraid to entrust our lives to Him. Sometimes people feel called to the priesthood but fear that it is too challenging and that they would fail to live out their commitment. We need to trust in the Lord. If He gives us a vocation, He will also give us the strength we need. Sometimes, very good candidates for the priesthood are overwhelmed by a sense of unworthiness. The Gospel should reassure us when we see how Jesus calls ordinary people to be His disciples. Some of them had histories that would seem to preclude a vocation. Levi, a publican, worked for the enemy, the Romans, and enriched himself by exploiting the poor. Saul, the Pharisee, persecuted the Church and even participated in the martyrdom of St. Stephen. Peter denied Jesus three times, intimidated not by a soldier with a lance but by a servant girl who noticed his accent. In all of these cases, faith in Christ and the power of His love sustained those who were called. It will be no different for you.

I hope Father Najim's *Radical Surrender: Letters to Seminarians* will help you to move further along the path of priestly formation. I pray that meditating upon this book will assist you in drawing closer to the Lord and to appropriate your vocation more deeply.

Sincerely yours in Christ,

+ /Jean, OfMCap

Sean Cardinal O'Malley, OFM Cap.
Archbishop of Boston

Dedication

To Father Mark Noonan, my seminary spiritual director,
through whom these lessons were learned.

Acknowledgments

This book would not have been possible without the help
and expertise of many people. I would like to thank Dea-
con James Keating and Jessi Kary, AO, at The Institute for
Priestly Formation for their willingness to publish this
manuscript and for their many suggestions which brought
greater clarity to the manuscript. I would also like to thank
Father John Horn, SJ, for his spiritual insights, many of
which I have incorporated into this book. Special thanks to
Father Bill Kelly for reviewing the manuscript and offering
helpful suggestions.

I owe a deep debt of gratitude to Patricia Skarda, profes-
sor of English at Smith College, for her skillful editing of
the manuscript.

The idea for this book came about when I began my ministry as Vocation Director for the Diocese of Providence and
formator at the Seminary of Our Lady of Providence. I am
continually inspired by the seminarians to whom I minister. I am grateful to each seminarian for his commitment to
growing in holiness. I am also grateful to my brother priests
who constantly challenge me to be the best priest I can be.
Last, but not least, I am grateful to my parents for being my
first teachers in the virtues of faith, hope, and charity and for
always supporting and encouraging me in my vocation.

How to Use This Book

In his book *Called to Communion*, then-Cardinal Joseph Ratzinger wrote, "The essential foundation of priestly ministry is a deep and personal bond to Jesus Christ. Everything hinges on this bond, and the heart of all preparation for priesthood ... must be an introduction to it."[1] While writing this book, I had one simple goal: to inspire the seminarian to enter deeply into this personal bond with Jesus Christ so that Christ can interiorly transform him. Seminary formation, in order to "work," must be interiorly appropriated; in other words, formation will be fruitful only if the seminarian allows Christ to transform his heart. Considering this transformation of the heart, I would like to propose how to receive the most from of this book. My desire is that this book will be an experience of prayer for you, a companion on your journey, not simply another book to read and then shelve.

Borrowing from the approach that *The Institute of Priestly Formation* takes each summer with its course material, I suggest that you read each letter in the style of *lectio divina.* Simply stated, read each letter prayerfully, and be attentive to the concepts or phrases that speak most deeply to your heart. Underlining key phrases or writing your thoughts in the margins may be helpful. As you read, keep in mind the important question, "What is the Lord saying to me?" At the end of each letter are questions to guide your prayer, and space is provided for you to write your thoughts, feelings, and desires in the form of a prayer to the Lord.

Practically speaking, here is what I envision:

- Take this book to the chapel during adoration of the Blessed Sacrament or to another quiet place of prayer. There, read one letter prayerfully, being attentive to the interior movements of grace in your heart (e.g., What is the Lord saying to me?). *Acknowledge* your feelings, thoughts, and desires, *relate* these in faith to Christ, *receive* what He wants to give, and *respond* in some way (more prayer, a particular action, etc.).[2]

- As you finish each letter, use the questions to lead you to an extended period of deeper prayer. If you do not need the questions, simply speak to the Lord about the thoughts, feelings, and desires that surfaced in your heart as you read.

- Use the space provided to write your prayer of desire to the Lord or the thoughts, feelings, and desires that came to you.

- Since each letter can serve as a springboard for spiritual direction, use the journal space to record important interior movements to discuss with your spiritual director.

Do not read this book quickly, cover to cover. Rather, read one letter at a time—daily, if possible. You may even feel called to read some letters more than once. After you have read each letter, you may feel called to go back and read the book again or to reread a certain letter that spoke powerfully to you. I also encourage you to dialogue with your vocation director about these letters and what the Lord is saying to you through them. Your vocation director is an important part of your seminary formation, and keeping him informed of your progress is important. Lastly, you may desire to use these letters in a discussion group with other seminarians. Oftentimes, the insights and graces the Lord gives to others can be an aid to deepen our own spiritual lives.

The Place of Encounter

My Dear Brother,

I am sitting in a coffee shop on the east side of Providence, Rhode Island, on a chilly, overcast Sunday afternoon in March. The sun has been making a valiant effort to break through the clouds, but it seems to be fighting a losing battle. Today I want the sun to stay behind the clouds, though: something happens to me, or rather within me, when the sun is behind the clouds. I feel more contemplative, reminded that the Son is within me.

The coffee shop is filled with university students studying, talking, surfing the Internet; some are holding hands and whispering to one another, looking closely into each other's eyes. How perfect that "I Only Have Eyes for You" is playing in the background. Every table and chair is taken. A young couple just left and gave me this perfect space by the window, complete with a nearby outlet for my laptop. As I stare out the window onto Thayer Street, cars are passing by; people are walking leisurely. Some are laughing; others look lost in their thoughts. One young man just kissed his girlfriend tenderly on the forehead. Some people are on their cell phones. Some seem disconnected from life, from their hearts, an emptiness in their eyes. What is happening in their hearts?

Today is one of those Sunday afternoons when I feel the need to get out, to be on my own, to write. I have wanted to write to you for some time, even though I know I will see you soon. My heart contains so much I want to share with you about the Lord, about the spiritual life, about what it means to be a good and holy priest, a spiritual father—not that I consider myself to be a holy priest, but in my heart, I *desire* to be, and I know that the Lord is calling me to be.

The coffee shop, the Internet, people, lovers, cars, cell phones—empty hearts. This does not seem like the ideal place to write about the spiritual life, about the seminary, about the priesthood; but, on second thought, maybe it is. Our culture militates against the silence for which the heart so deeply longs, the silence into which Christ is inviting you. You have been called by God to the priesthood. You have been called out of your family, out of your parish community, and out of this culture, precisely so that you can be sent back to your family, to the Church community, and to the culture to bring Christ to them. You know that the heart longs for silence; you know what having silence in your heart is like, to be alone with the Lord, or you would not have heard His voice calling you to be in the seminary. You also know the battle of keeping your heart united to Christ. I want to invite you to enter deeply into your heart, not to be self-absorbed or introspective, but to encounter the Lord, who lives within you. As the *Catechism of the Catholic Church* states, the heart is "the place of encounter" (2563). Allow Christ to form your heart.

Too many people are disconnected from their hearts, and thus from where Christ wants to encounter them. Too many priests and seminarians are disconnected from their hearts or do not know how, or have forgotten how, to connect to them. Christ dwells in our heart, and we will encounter Him there—but only if we have the courage to go there.

Particular interior habits will help you to stay intimately united to Christ in your heart if you will only take the time to form them, or, more accurately, if you allow the Holy Spirit to form them in you. The seminary provides the perfect time and space to form these habits. By living these interior habits, you will be deeply rooted in Christ and will build a strong foundation for your priesthood. Let the Lord speak to your heart; expect the Lord to act in you. These letters contain the words and insights that the Lord has given to me; now, I share them with you. My desire for you is that as you read, your heart will be set aflame with the grace of the Holy Spirit.

Well, my coffee is almost finished and is not as hot as it was when I started writing ... time for another cup.

With prayer,

Father Najim

Trust

*"By faith Abraham obeyed when he was called to go out
to a place that he was to receive as an inheritance;
he went out, not knowing where he was to go."*
Heb. 11:8

My Dear Brother,

For the last couple of weeks, I have wanted to write to you. As I said, the conversation at the table lifted my spirits; but when you and I spoke privately, I sensed that you are a bit unsettled, that you are questioning yourself.

Let me assure you that I truly believe that you made the right decision to enter the seminary. Your decision really is a win-win scenario. During your time at the seminary, either your call to the priesthood will be confirmed and deepened, or you will come to see that you are called to another vocation. Either way, as you open yourself to the Holy Spirit, you will see more clearly why you were created. Should not every person desire to know God's plan for his or her life? Your time in the seminary will be some of the most transformative years of your life: a time to deepen your relationship with Christ and the Church, a time to form lasting spiritual friendships.

If my instinct was right and you are indeed feeling a bit unsettled, ask yourself a question: *Why did I enter the seminary in the first place?* You allowed the Lord to lead you to the seminary because you believe in your heart that He is calling you to be a priest, plain and simple. True, you may have experienced some interior turbulence before you entered the seminary, and some even now, but recall why you initially came to the seminary: *I am here because I believe God is calling me to be a priest.* Even still, there may be moments when you may find yourself asking some questions: *How in the world did I end up here? Why has the Lord led me here?* Like St. Thomas the Apostle, you might find yourself praying, "*Master ... how can [I] know the way?*" (Jn. 14:5) By now, in your conversations with your brother seminarians, you have learned that each man has his own unique vocation story. But the truth is that for each of us, the journey began in the same way: we were mysteriously drawn to the priesthood in our hearts. At some point, you began to experience an attraction to the priestly life. Eventually, you began to seriously think about this attraction. Some men started thinking about it at an early age, others, after a conversion experience, still others in the midst of a career. Regardless of each man's story, all of you took the same road: you made the life-altering decision to enter this place called "the seminary."

Those thoughts, which began in our minds, eventually took root in our hearts. Then, they became the heart of our prayer. In your personal prayer, I hope you have come to understand that it was not you who created those thoughts of a vocation; it was the Holy Spirit prompting you, inviting you to embark upon this marvelous journey. Truly, a magnificent spiritual discovery occurs in understanding that the origin of every priestly vocation is in the heart of God, and yet *our* hearts become the place where the Spirit begins this work. When we truly ponder our calling, we can exclaim with St. Paul, *"Oh, the depth of the riches and wisdom and knowledge of God! How inscrutable are his judgments and how unsearchable his ways!"* (Romans 11:33).

Your decision to enter the seminary proves that you already understand the foundation of formation—trust. You decided to enter the seminary because you believed that the Lord was leading you there. You entered because that decision resonated with your prayerful spirit. You believe that your attraction to the priesthood was inspired by the Holy Spirit and that the Lord Jesus invited you to place your trust in Him and to take action. You obeyed the call to go where the Lord was leading you, even though, like Abraham, you did not have the map in front of you. The bottom line is that you trusted, and now, trust must become habitual for you. Trust in the Lord must be rooted deep within your heart because it is the sure foundation of formation and a necessary virtue for the priestly life.

Consider St. Joseph. He is a model of trust. The Gospel stories about Joseph so clearly indicate that he placed his absolute trust in the Lord. Once the Lord spoke to him, he did not question; he simply acted. God said, "Joseph, son of David, do not be afraid to take Mary your wife into your home" (Mt. 1:20). So, Joseph chose not to be afraid, and he took Mary into his home. Then God said, "Rise, take the child and his mother, flee to Egypt" (Mt. 2:13). So, Joseph rose and took Jesus and Mary to Egypt. He did not question; he just acted. He placed his trust in God.

Reflection on the Gospel story about Joseph taking Jesus and Mary to Egypt was a turning point in my discernment. Before I decided to enter the seminary, I worked as youth minister in a parish. I used to go into the Church to spend some time in prayer before I went to my office. One day, I was meditating on this particular Gospel, and the Lord acted. He made it clear to me that Joseph did not hesitate when the angel told him to take action; He made it clear to me that He was asking me to take action, to make the decision to enter the seminary. I made the decision, and the Lord has not let me down.

You can also consider a more modern example of acting on God's word: the story of Blessed Mother Teresa of Calcutta. While studying and teaching in India, she witnessed tremendous poverty. On September 10, 1946, she was on a train ride from Calcutta to Darjeeling for a spiritual retreat. During this train ride, the Lord spoke very clearly to her about the mission to the poorest of the poor for which He had prepared her. This experience, mystical in character, was a defining moment in her life. Without questioning the Lord, she responded to His invitation. She left the community of the Sisters of Our Lady of Loreto and founded the Missionaries of Charity. Mother Teresa trusted the Lord unconditionally. She did not see everything that the Lord had in store for her future, but she always trusted that He had called her and given her this particular mission.

My brother, as you journey through your seminary formation, I encourage you to ponder the words the Lord spoke to the prophet Jeremiah: "For I know well the plans I have in mind for you, says the Lord, plans for your welfare, not for woe! plans to give you a future full of hope" (Jer. 29:11). In theology class you will learn about God's divine providence, His wisdom, which governs creation; in your prayer, you will see more and more clearly that God has a particular plan for every human life. Learn to apply the theological truth of God's providence to your own life. In other words, believing that God has a particular plan for *you* is vital.

Be at peace. "Peace be with you," said Christ to His fearful disciples (Jn. 20:19). True, there may be times when you do not see as clearly as you want to see. Maybe you have had doubts, or you are uncertain about your decision and your future. Trust. Be at peace. The virtue of faith is important here: "Faith is the realization of what is hoped for and evidence of things not seen" (Heb. 11:1). Remember, this virtue of faith was given to you at Baptism; you already possess this amazing gift of faith in your soul. The more you exercise it, the more it grows. To be a priest, you must be a man of faith because you need to inspire others to live in faith and trust.

Like St. Joseph and Blessed Mother Teresa, learn to live in God's providence. Simply put, if you believe that the Lord led you to the seminary, now also believe that He will continue to lead you to ordination and in your life as a priest. My trust in the Lord continues to grow stronger and stronger because I see how He continually leads me, even though I do not always see the way clearly before me. So, let trust, deeply rooted in your heart, become a defining habit in your life. Remember the prayer that St. Faustina exclaimed: "*Jesus, I trust in you.*" Pray these words often, and remember that when you exercise the virtue of trust in the Lord, you are imitating the saints—you are imitating St. Joseph and Blessed Mother Teresa. If you read the lives of the saints, you will never find one who did not have tremendous trust and confidence in the Lord. You will never find a saint who did not believe that the Lord was leading him or her every step of the way, even though each may have struggled at times.

The most basic lesson that I have ever learned is that trust is the foundation of formation. You will experience challenging times in seminary, but trust in the Lord. He has led you here. You are where He wants you to be. Live each day with that conviction.

With prayer for your growth in trust,

Father Najim

Questions for Prayer

Do I truly believe that the Lord has led me here and that He will continue to lead me?

What can I do on a practical level that will strengthen the virtue of trust in my heart?

The thoughts, feelings, and desires that surfaced as I read this letter:

My prayer:

Radical Surrender

"Father ... not my will but yours be done."
Lk. 22:42

My Dear Brother,

I hope my insights on trust were helpful to you. I do understand the sentiment one seminarian expressed when he wrote, "I know when I trust I am imitating the saints, but I'm no St. Joseph." True, when we look within ourselves, we feel completely beneath the standard of the saints; but we are called to become saints. When we contemplate their lives, we see a common thread: they completely surrendered to the Lord. We are called to surrender our lives to Him, as well, in a radical way.

I remember a specific moment when this call to surrender became a deep reality for me. During my time in the seminary, I often went at night to the chapel for quiet prayer. I remember one night when I was experiencing a particular interior struggle. I was unsure that this was the road the Lord had chosen for me. I was struggling because even if this was the road, I was not sure I was *ready* to take it, or even if I *wanted* to take it. What was I to do? So, in the dimly-lit chapel, I knelt in prayer on the marble sanctuary step in front of the altar, and I poured my heart out: *Lord, whatever you want me to be, I will be; whatever you want me to do, I will do; wherever you want me to go, I will go. I surrender to you; I am yours.* Praying those heartfelt words, I experienced a profound inner peace. I did not receive a revelation, but in praying from the depths of my heart, I knew that the Lord would continue to lead me. We receive true peace and freedom when we surrender ourselves to the Lord.

I challenge you to look into your heart and pray: *Lord, what are you asking of me during this time in the seminary? What will you ask of me throughout my life as a priest?* If you listen quietly, you will hear Him speak to you: *Give me your heart.* As you grow in prayer, as you practice the interior habit of trust, you will find a desire growing within you—the desire to surrender yourself to Jesus Christ. This desire to surrender your life to Christ is the Holy Spirit working in your heart, drawing you closer to the One to whom you will be configured on the day of your ordination. Do not be afraid of this invitation from the Holy Spirit. The act of surrendering your life to Christ is unquestionably one of the most important moments in your spiritual life; but more than a single moment, it is an interior habit that needs to be formed in you so that you can live this radical surrender daily.

If you think about it, this habit of surrender is so important in the life of the priest that the Church ritualizes it in the Rite of Ordination. On your ordination day, you will literally lie prostrate on the floor as an act of surrendering your life to Christ for the good of the Church. This act of prostration is an exterior sign of an interior reality. True, at the time of your ordination, you will be physically prostrate; but more importantly, you should have already surrendered your will to Christ by the time you reach that point. No, you will not be perfectly surrendered, but the habit should be strong. Your ordination day should not be the first time that you lie prostrate, nor should it be the last.

Let me share a story about Pope John Paul II as a young priest in Poland. While with friends on a canoeing vacation, Father Wojtyla was summoned to Warsaw by Cardinal Wyszynski. When Father Wojtyla arrived, the Cardinal informed Father Wojtyla that he was to be consecrated auxiliary bishop. After Father Wojtyla said *yes*—*yes* to the Lord was habitual in him—he went to a nearby convent chapel to pray. The sisters of that convent later recounted how Father Wojtyla had lain prostrate for hours on the chapel floor. His life was already surrendered to the Lord Jesus, yet he felt the need to surrender more deeply at that moment. What a tremendous lesson for us! We are never completely surrendered to Christ; He is always inviting us to a more radical surrender.

The paradox of the Christian life is this: only when we surrender our lives to the Lord are we truly free. We will experience true freedom only when we completely give ourselves to Jesus Christ. When we surrender, we let go of everything that keeps us from belonging completely to Jesus Christ; we let go of our own will and open ourselves completely to God's will. But let us be honest; this invitation to surrender to the Lord may cause some fear because we cannot see the future. We do not know what lies ahead. With trust, however, we have no reason to fear.

When we are afraid to surrender, it is helpful for us to meditate on the experience of Jesus in the Garden of Gethsemane. In His humanity, Jesus experienced fear; but in that same moment, Christ gained for us the strength to overcome the temptation to fear: "Father ... not my will but yours be done" (Lk. 22:42). In these words, we contemplate Jesus surrendering to the Father. This prayer of Christ must be deeply rooted in our hearts so that our will can be conformed to His.

To be a seminarian, to be a priest, you must first be a disciple. To be a disciple means freely choosing to follow Christ wherever He leads you. I encourage you to pray this prayer often:

> *Lord Jesus, whatever you want me to be, I will be; wherever you want me to go, I will go. I surrender my life to you; give me your grace and show me the way.*

I exhort you to pray these words because this is precisely the kind of interior disposition you must have as a priest. You must be willing to go wherever the Lord leads you, remembering that your life is not your own but is at the service of Jesus Christ and His Bride, the Church. If you are not willing to go wherever the Lord leads you—any parish, any assignment—then you must focus on building this habit of surrender.

I remember sitting in the rector's office when I was a seminarian, speaking to him about some spiritual struggles. He looked at me and said, "Michael, rest in the Lord." He then gave me a little book of meditations by John Henry Cardinal Newman entitled, *Lead, Kindly Light*. The title of the book is taken from a poem that Newman wrote, which became a source of great consolation for me. I share it with you now, hoping that it brings you the same light and peace it brought me.

Lead, Kindly Light, amid the encircling gloom,
Lead Thou me on!
The night is dark, and I am far from home—
Lead Thou me on!
Keep Thou my feet; I do not ask to see
The distant scene,—one step enough for me.

I was not ever thus, nor pray'd that Thou
Shouldst lead me on.
I lov'd to choose and see my path; but now
Lead Thou me on!
I lov'd the garish day, and, spite of fears,
Pride rul'd my will: remember not past years.

So long Thy power hath bless'd me, sure it still
Will lead me on,
O'er moor and fen, o'er crag and torrent, till
The night is gone;
And with the morn those angel faces smile
Which I have lov'd long since, and lost awhile.

With prayer for your radical surrender,

Father Najim

Questions for Prayer

How deeply have I entered into my surrender to the Lord Jesus?

What is holding me back from more radically surrendering to the Lord?

The thoughts, feelings, and desires that surfaced as I read this letter:

My prayer:

The Lordship of Christ

"Jesus Christ is Lord."
Phil. 2:11

My Dear Brother,

People are often surprised when I tell them that, except for some prayers, I did not learn Latin in the seminary and have no proficiency in the language now. I did, however, learn one very simple Latin lesson: the word *Lord* comes from the Latin *dominus,* from which the English word *dominion* is derived. *What is the point of this ever-so-brief Latin lesson?* Simple. The spiritual life follows a logical sequence: Trust in the Lord leads us to surrender to Him; and when we surrender to Him, we allow Him to have dominion in our lives. We allow Him to be Lord of our lives.

Those charged with your formation breathe together in the service of a vital goal: Your years in the seminary are meant to *change you for the good*; and to be changed, you must be formed. The question that you need to ask is: *Who is forming me?* True, those in charge of your formation are the priests and others appointed by the bishop, but the one who ultimately forms you interiorly is the Lord Jesus Christ.

Formation means giving Jesus Christ dominion over every area of your life and living under His Lordship. Does this concept sound excessive to you? To those who do not understand life in Christ, it may sound excessive; but to those who understand that being truly human means living in Christ, this is precisely the call. In fact, to allow Christ to be Lord of our lives means to live in the fullness of freedom. "For freedom Christ set us free" (Gal. 5:1).

Now, admittedly, submitting ourselves to the Lordship of Christ is easier said than done. In fact, sometimes our nature—thanks to original sin—is to rebel against authority. But the authority of Christ does not oppress; it liberates. The authority of Christ does not hinder our growth; it enables us to flourish in virtue and holiness. Remember, His "yoke is easy" and His "burden light" (Mt. 11:30).

One of my favorite saints is Ignatius of Loyola, the great founder of the Society of Jesus and an important saint for seminarians and priests. He was dedicated to helping priests grow strong in their interior lives. St. Ignatius understood the meaning of living under Christ's Lordship. In his classic *Spiritual Exercises*, he proposes *A Meditation on Two Standards* (week 2, day 4): the one standard of Jesus Christ, whom he calls our "supreme Captain and Lord"; the other of Satan, whom he calls "the mortal enemy of our human nature." Because he was a soldier, Ignatius approached this meditation with all the passion of a man prepared for battle. In the first part of the meditation, Ignatius has us visualize Satan, sitting on a great throne of fire and smoke. Satan calls together demons and delivers a speech to them, exhorting them to tempt people with the lust of riches, which leads to pride, and ultimately every other vice.

In the second part of the meditation, Ignatius invites us to visualize Christ in a "lowly place." He tells us that Christ is "beautiful and gracious to behold." In the meditation, Jesus chooses His disciples and sends them on a mission to proclaim His message, which is the opposite of Satan's. Christ's disciples invite people to embrace poverty and humility, which lead to all other virtues. To end the meditation, Ignatius invites us to enter into prayerful conversation with the Blessed Virgin Mary, asking her to obtain from Christ the grace to live under His standard. To live under Christ's standard was St. Ignatius's desire for himself, his followers, and, indeed, for every Christian; it was his goal in writing *The Spiritual Exercises*. He knew that in order to be holy, he needed to surrender himself to the dominion of Jesus Christ.

But how does living according to the standard of Christ translate into our everyday lives? In order for Jesus to be Lord of our lives, we need to give Him dominion over every area of our lives. We need to heed the advice of St. Paul, who tells us to offer our *bodies* to the Lord as a living sacrifice (Rom. 12:1). He also tells us that our bodies are temples of the Holy Spirit (1 Cor. 6:19). You may have heard that the body is a good servant but a bad master. That is true. Our bodies can be rebellious when it comes to the spiritual life: We give in to laziness, lust, gluttony, and a whole host of other bodily cravings. Our bodies should serve us, not rule us. The challenge for you in formation—and beyond—is to learn how to let Christ rule your body by staying affectively united to Him, by staying close to Him in your heart.

What does it mean to be affectively united to Christ? It means that you allow the grace of Christ to transform even your passions and emotional life. Emotions can sometimes get the best of us. We need to learn to live in union with Jesus, to allow our emotions to be tutored by His grace.

Allowing Christ to tutor our emotions is most important for celibacy and is one of the reasons why mortification is a good practice. When we choose not to allow our negative emotions and passions to govern us, we need to turn to something—Someone, rather—to empower us. We turn to Christ and unite ourselves to Him; we say to Him, "Be the Lord of my life." Is Christ the Lord of your body and emotions? Do you believe that you are mature in your emotional life? Do you lose your temper often? Do you easily give in to sadness? Does the power of lust often control you? Your growth in self-knowledge is important. Learn to unite yourself to Christ in all of these areas. He will help you; He will strengthen you (cf. Is. 41:10).

Just as Christ must be the Lord of our bodies, so must he reign over our minds and spirits. What does it mean that Christ has dominion over our *minds*? St. Paul writes: "Do not conform yourselves to this age but be transformed by the renewal of your mind, that you may discern what is the will of God, what is good and pleasing and perfect" (Rom. 12:2). The mind is very powerful; it can be filled with the loftiest spiritual thoughts or focused on the basest aspects of human life. The challenge for you is to allow Christ to rule your mind, as St. Paul challenged the Philippians: "Finally, brothers, whatever is true, whatever is honorable, whatever is just, whatever is pure, whatever is lovely, whatever is gracious, if there is any excellence and if there is anything worthy of praise, think about these things" (4:8). This remarkable exhortation is indicative as to what happens when we allow Christ to be Lord over our thoughts. If we allow Christ to be Lord of our minds, His grace will necessarily change our behaviors.

And, my brother, Christ must be Lord of your *spirit*. Simply put, you must learn to love prayer so that your spirit will be drawn to the Lord more and more. If the spirit is weak, then everything else will be weak; but if the spirit is strong, then the entirety of our lives will be strong. When we allow Christ to be Lord of our spirit, we radiate His presence to others. People see Christ in us. We become a bridge for others to encounter the Lord. When He is Lord of our spirit, we are not conquered by sadness or pessimism; rather, we radiate the fruits of the Holy Spirit.

The task of the priest is to proclaim Jesus Christ as Lord. Our message is only as authentic as our life. If Christ is Lord of our life, we will effectively invite people into friendship with Him; if He is not Lord of our life, our message will be ineffective.

Learn to be weak with Christ. Remember our Lord's words to St. Paul, "My grace is sufficient for you, for power is made perfect in weakness" (2 Cor. 12:9). I know that you desire Christ to be Lord of your life, and I also know your frustration with your imperfections. Let Christ show you your faults, and let Him heal them for His glory. We are imperfect. Such surrender is a struggle; but we must persevere in the struggle, for the struggle is precisely what makes room for Christ to reign. In Christ, we are strong. So, my brother, let Him reign in you!

With prayer in the struggle,

Father Najim

Questions for Prayer

In what particular area(s) of my life do I need to give dominion to Christ?

On a practical level, what can I do on a daily basis to make
sure that my emotions and passions do not control me?

The thoughts, feelings, and desires that surfaced as I read
this letter:

My prayer:

Humility and Openness

*"Whoever exalts himself will be humbled;
but whoever humbles himself will be exalted."*
Mt. 23:12

My Dear Brother,

I understand that you have encountered other seminarians who have told you that the faculty is playing a game with you. These seminarians have told you that the seminary is filled with hoops through which you need to jump. Truthfully, I am surprised you did not hear this rumor sooner. Some seminarians believe that the faculty—or even their vocation director—is out to get them, that they are constantly being watched for the smallest slip-up. Some men will do nothing but complain about the formation program and the faculty. They will tell you how they cannot wait to be ordained and shake the seminary dust from their feet, acting as if they have more priestly experience than all the priest-faculty in the seminary combined.

Warning: Guard yourself against this attitude, and do not permit it to infect you. Instead, have the mind of Christ, "Who, though he was in the form of God, did not regard equality with God something to be grasped. Rather, he emptied himself, taking the form of a slave, coming in human likeness; and found human in appearance, he humbled himself" (Phil. 2:6-8).

Honestly, some seminarians really believe that those in charge of their formation want them to fail. If a man is consistently closed to correction, constantly complaining about everything, the real issue is in his own heart, not in the formation program. And if he is constantly complaining, the faculty has the right to challenge him. The last thing the priesthood needs is men who spend their days complaining instead of attending to the work needing to be done in the Lord's vineyard. But let us be honest: some seminarians—and, yes, some priests, as well—have a complete lack of humility and openness. They believe that they know better than priests who have been ordained for many years, priests who have pastoral experience, priests who are ultimately trying to help them to be the best future priests they can be.

Two of the most important dispositions you can foster in your heart are humility and openness to the Holy Spirit working through those charged with your formation. Contrary to what some may believe, the formation program is not crafted to make you weak or to take away your freedom; rather, the purpose of the formation program is to challenge you to grow in all areas of formation—human, spiritual, intellectual, and pastoral—so that you can be strengthened and grow in freedom.

Yes, you will be challenged. We are all imperfect; we all have rough edges. And when the faculty perceive a rough edge in you, they have every right—indeed, every obligation—to challenge you to polish the edge into a smooth texture. You are being formed to be a priest of Jesus Christ, another Christ to the people of God. The people need a man who has been formed in virtue and is living in holiness, not a man who is driven by his own agenda. Although priest faculty are imperfect, they generally have enough pastoral experience to know what works and what does not work, what quirks drive people away and what traits draw people to Christ.

I remember a time in the seminary when I was challenged because I loved engaging in political debates. I enjoyed pushing the buttons of men who disagreed with me. I was not corrected for having an interest in politics but because I was not always open to listening to the other side. We are not called to compromise our beliefs, but we are called to listen to what others have to say. Common sense tells us that people will be more apt to listen to us if they know that we are really listening to them. Ironically, the challenge regarding political debates came through a peer evaluation—another great grace in the seminary. When a brother seminarian cares enough about you to challenge you to work on something that may be an obstacle in your formation, consider thanking him.

Openness to truth is one of the most important dispositions we can have in the seminary and in our priesthood. Openness to feedback is good and healthy. In fact, we should desire to know where we can grow; we should want to know the areas where we can improve. We should welcome challenges and suggestions from faculty and our brother seminarians. After ordination, seeking feedback is very important. Do not be afraid to ask for feedback from your pastor, your brother priests, and even from a couple of close spiritual friends.

Instead of judging the men who complain and gripe, be a light to them. Choose not to complain; choose not to be negative or cynical. Complaints and cynicism are poisons that can destroy our hearts and infect others. Rather, be open to the challenges that are posed to you in formation. Pray for the virtue of humility to be alive in your heart so that you can be open to growing in the ways that Christ desires.

I want to share with you a most beautiful prayer called the "Litany of Humility," written by Cardinal Merry del Val, Secretary of State for Pope Pius X. Say this prayer with your heart, and live it in your daily life:

> *O Jesus! meek and humble of heart,* **Hear me.**
> *From the desire of being esteemed,* **Deliver me, Jesus.**
> *From the desire of being loved ...*
> *From the desire of being extolled ...*
> *From the desire of being honored ...*
> *From the desire of being praised ...*
> *From the desire of being preferred to others ...*
> *From the desire of being consulted ...*
> *From the desire of being approved ...*
> *From the fear of being humiliated ...*
> *From the fear of being despised ...*
> *From the fear of suffering rebukes ...*
> *From the fear of being calumniated ...*
> *From the fear of being forgotten ...*
> *From the fear of being ridiculed ...*
> *From the fear of being wronged ...*
> *From the fear of being suspected ...*
> *That others may be loved more than I,*
> **Jesus, grant me the grace to desire it.**

That others may be esteemed more than I ...
That, in the opinion of the world,
*   others may increase and I may decrease ...*
That others may be chosen and I set aside ...
That others may be praised and I unnoticed ...
That others may be preferred to me in everything ...
That others may become holier than I, provided that
*   I may become as holy as I should ...*

With prayer for openness and humility,

Father Najim

Questions for Prayer

Where do I need to be more open to truth in my formation?

In what practical ways can I foster a deeper humility and openness to truth in my life?

The thoughts, feelings, and desires that surfaced as I read this letter:

My prayer:

Prayer

"Pray without ceasing."
1 Thes. 5:17

My Dear Brother,

Hopefully, the rhythm of prayer that is such an integral part of seminary life is becoming more natural. Praying Morning and Evening Prayer in community, as well as attending daily Mass, has the power to focus to your day. The structure of community prayer can deepen the habit of personal prayer in your life; and of all of the habits that I encourage you to form while in the seminary, praying must be the strongest because in prayer you will receive the strength to live your life as a priest. In prayer you will receive the grace to live the promises you make on your ordination day. In prayer you will be given the grace to acquire and grow in the virtues necessary to be a holy priest. Prayer must be the air you breathe, your lifeblood. The bottom line is this: you cannot be a good seminarian or a good priest if you do not pray well.

While structured prayer in the seminary community is vital, more is needed to cultivate a strong spiritual life. Perhaps you believe that your personal prayer life should be much deeper than it is now, but you are not quite sure how to make it so. Prayer is about deepening your friendship with Jesus. If love unites friends, then prayer is essentially about love. Prayer is about the union of our hearts, minds, and wills with the heart, mind, and will of Christ. Prayer is not so much about *doing* as it is about *listening*. Prayer is about receiving and being received, allowing the Holy Spirit to pray in us, "for we do not know how to pray as we ought, but the Spirit itself intercedes with inexpressible groanings" (Rom. 8:26).

How should you pray outside of community prayer? As you know, each person is drawn to different forms of prayer. Certain fundamentals, however, are present in all authentic prayer. First and foremost, our prayer must be from our hearts, and our hearts must be engaged in our prayer. Prayer is literally having a "heart-to-heart" conversation with the Lord. When we speak about love, we often speak about the heart. Let your prayer flow from your heart to the heart of Christ; let Christ communicate the love of His heart to your heart. Yes, you must know that Christ loves you personally.

One of the most helpful images for personal prayer, especially for the seminarian and priest, is from John 13. This is one of my favorite scenes in the Scripture. In this Gospel scene, Jesus is celebrating the Last Supper with His disciples, and He knows that Judas is about to betray Him. Christ startles His apostles with the words, "One of you will betray me" (Jn. 13:21). In that moment, Peter signals to John, the Beloved Disciple, to ask our Lord who will betray Him. Then, we see one of the most significant scenes in all of Scripture regarding prayer: John, the Beloved Disciple, rests his head on Jesus' chest and asks Him who His betrayer will be.

My brother, contemplate this scene: the Beloved Disciple listening to the innermost Being of God, close to Him, resting his head on Jesus' heart. Can you see yourself there? Can you put yourself in John's place? This is where Jesus desires you to be because this is where He lives ... resting against the innermost Being of the Father (cf. Jn. 1:18). Let Him take you there as well. This is the starting point of your prayer, resting on the heart of Christ, allowing yourself to be embraced by Him.

As a seminarian, you need to be able to see yourself resting in the arms of Christ, resting your head on His chest, listening to His heart beat in love—for you. Yes, you must have that kind of familiarity with Jesus, and you will acquire this familiarity with Jesus in deep, heart-to-heart prayer. Only when your prayer is deep and from the heart will you be comfortable in the arms of Christ.

If you think this talk about "resting in the arms of Christ" seems too poetic, remember that it was not too poetic for the Beloved Disciple. He knew Jesus so intimately that he was comfortable to rest in Him, even *on* Him. Remember you are praying to Jesus Christ our Savior. Do not hold on to shames or fears that can prevent you from receiving love from His heart. Your desire must be to know, love, and serve Christ. Only in prayer do you come to know Jesus more intimately, to love Him more deeply, and to desire to serve Him more fervently. And only in prayer will you truly come to know yourself, too.

Our beloved, late Holy Father, Pope John Paul II, gave the Church a spiritual program to follow for the Third Millennium: to contemplate the face of Jesus with Mary as

51

our guide. In your prayer, seeing the face of Jesus is important. You must enter into His Paschal Mystery. Thus, reading and praying with the Gospels is vital. Read the Gospels, and allow them be the content of your prayer. See yourself in the Gospel scenes: see yourself in the place of the first apostles, who heard the call of the Lord, "Come after me, and I will make you fishers of men" (Mt. 4:19); see yourself as the leper in need of healing; see yourself as the Beloved Disciple at the foot of the cross, looking upon Christ crucified. Enter into these scenes and let Christ speak to you, heart to heart. This is true prayer; this is prayer that will transform you and make your heart like Christ's.

So, while prayer in community is important, set time aside every day to enter into deep, personal prayer with the Lord. If you do, you will find a few things happening. First, you will discover in your heart an increased desire to pray and to spend time with Jesus. Second, you will be more deeply aware of His presence in your daily life. Third, you will realize the fruits of the Holy Spirit coming to life in you. And when the fruits of the Holy Spirit are alive in us, people are attracted to Christ through our witness. Prayer is not just for you; your prayer leads others to Jesus. Finally, the communal prayer in which you participate will become richer, more intimate, as you receive the love of Christ and share in the fellowship of common faith you have with other seminarians.

Be patient in your prayer. Some days, you will want to keep praying because you are experiencing the nearness of the Lord; other days, your mind will be filled with distractions, and you will feel that the Lord is a million miles away. Do not base your prayer on your feelings, but let faith-filled feelings lead you to the foundation of prayer—communion with Christ. The Lord is always with you. The important thing is that you set time aside every day to be alone with Him.

With prayer for your prayer,

Father Najim

Questions for Prayer

In what way am I being invited to devote myself to deep prayer with the Lord outside of structured community prayer?

Can I imagine myself in the arms of Jesus, listening to His heart love me? If not, what is blocking my reception of His love in this way?

The thoughts, feelings, and desires that surfaced as I read this letter:

My prayer:

Honesty and Spiritual Direction

"The truth will set you free."
Jn. 8:32

My Dear Brother,

Initial hesitation in opening your heart to your spiritual director is normal, particularly concerning the dark and wounded areas of your life. We can easily talk about all that is going well, but entrusting the whole of our hearts is often more difficult. In exposing the darkness of our lives to the light of Christ, however, enables Him to shine in us; by revealing our wounds, we experience the Lord's healing.

I saw this truth concretely in the recent illness of my brother-in-law, who ended up in the hospital and learned that he had eighty percent blockage in four arteries in his heart—a life-threatening condition, to say the least. Though he had been experiencing warning signs of a heart condition for a while, he generally ignored the symptoms. Only when he experienced tremendous pain did he act; only when he faced the truth was he able to be healed.

Jesus tells us in the Gospel of John that "the truth will set you free" (Jn. 8:32). If we are honest with ourselves, we know when something is physically wrong with us. We have all had that experience: our bodies tell us, through pain, that something is not right. Our bodies try to tell us the truth, but we want to bury the truth by pretending that something else is happening, something temporary, not a big deal. When we finally accept the truth, we go to the doctor, hoping we can begin to heal. Should we not treat our spiritual health in the same manner as our physical health?

The truth will set us free. One of the most important journeys you can make during your time in the seminary is the journey into your heart—a heroic, courageous journey to the place of encounter, a journey where you are willing to confront whatever you will find. My brother, think about all the masks we wear. We do our best to hide our brokenness and our wounds. We pretend we are okay when we know that something is not quite right inside of us. Why do we do this? Because sometimes we are afraid of the truth, afraid to journey into the heart because of what we will find. We must overcome precisely this fear so that we can experience the interior healing and liberation that the Holy Spirit desires to bring us. The Church, in Her wisdom, has provided spiritual directors to us in seminary formation to accompany us on this important interior journey.

Honesty is one of the most important aspects of your formation: honesty with the Lord, with yourself, and with your spiritual director. Sure, I know that most of what you are experiencing in formation is good, grace-filled, and holy. But darkness dwells in each one of us, and only by exposing that darkness to the light of Christ will we be able to receive His healing. Only when we are willing to stand spiritually naked before the Lord— and our director—can we experience the true power of the Holy Spirit.

I remember having a conversation with another seminarian when we were together in formation. We shared the same spiritual director, a priest for whom we both had tremendous love and respect. This seminarian told me something that has always stuck with me. He said, "Whenever you're in spiritual direction and you're tempted *not* to say something to your director, it's exactly *that* which you should say." That is excellent advice. St. Josemaría Escrivá gives us similar advice: "Don't hide those suggestions of the devil from your director. When you confide them to him, your victory brings you more grace from God. Moreover, you now have the gift of counsel and the prayers of your spiritual father to help you keep right on conquering."[3] We should not be afraid to share anything with our spiritual director. The Holy Spirit will speak through him. The Lord works in amazing ways in spiritual direction when we are honest about our wounds. This exhortation is also true regarding the Sacrament of Reconciliation, which ought to be a consistent part of your spiritual life. When we expose *our* wounds, we are receptive to the healing that flows from *His* wounds.

My brother, continue to be honest with yourself: Are you afraid to take a deep, honest look into your heart, into your life? Are you afraid to enter into the wounds of your soul? Is there something you are hiding from your spiritual director, something that you are afraid to reveal? Remember, that is *exactly* what you should reveal. If you are afraid, pray to have the courage of the three young men in the fiery furnace (Dan. 3). Recall their story. Because they refused to worship a golden statue, King Nebuchadnezzar had them cast into the fiery furnace. In fact, he had the furnace heated seven times hotter than usual. The three young men went, without fear, into the fiery furnace. And what happened?

The Son of God was with them. Remember, when we journey into our souls, we are not alone. Christ is with us. In fact, when we take a long, hard, honest look into our wounded hearts, we find Him, waiting to heal us, even to embrace us.

Do not be afraid. The truth will set you free.

With prayer for freedom in truth,

Father Najim

Questions for Prayer

How does the Holy Spirit work in and through my spiritual director?

What area(s) of my life do I need to bring to direction that I have been afraid to talk about?

The thoughts, feelings, and desires that surfaced as I read this letter:

My prayer:

The Eucharist

"Jesus said to them, 'I am the bread of life;
whoever comes to me will never hunger,
and whoever believes in me will never thirst."
Jn. 6:35

My Dear Brother,

One of the great blessings of living in the seminary is the gift of daily Mass and the presence of the Eucharist where you live. To have the opportunity to stop in and visit Our Lord in the tabernacle, even if just for a few moments, in the midst of a hectic day is a great grace. Finding yourself desiring to spend more time with our eucharistic Lord is a great sign of growth in your vocation. Cultivate this desire in your heart.

The topic of the Eucharist is inexhaustible but, in this letter, I desire to share some thoughts with you about love for the Eucharist and why the Eucharist must be at the center of your life as a seminarian and as a priest. Certainly, you will study eucharistic theology in the seminary. My point here is not so much to give you a theology lesson as to encourage you to grow in your love for and devotion to Jesus Christ in the Blessed Sacrament.

To begin, then, I invite you to ponder this reality: there is no Eucharist without the priesthood. God created you to be a priest; therefore, the very reason you exist is for the Eucharist. You exist for the Eucharist. You exist so that

Christ can continue to abide sacramentally with His Church until the end of time. Although, as a priest, you will do many other things besides celebrating Mass, the Eucharist is the heart of the Church and the priesthood. The Eucharist, therefore, must be at the core of your heart.

As a priest—as a seminarian—you must be a man of the Eucharist. Everything you do must flow from the Eucharist, and everything you experience on a daily basis must be brought back to the Eucharist. Much of my own discernment prior to entering the seminary occurred in prayer before the Blessed Sacrament. I vividly remember one morning, making a holy hour in the presence of Our Lord; He was clearly inviting me to enter the seminary. I know the Lord could have spoken to my heart even if I were not in His eucharistic presence, but something about being in the presence of the Lord helps me to listen more attentively to Him and to keep my focus on His abiding presence in my life.

Now, if the priest exists for the Eucharist, then your life must be intimately united to Jesus Christ in the Blessed Sacrament. For you to form a strong eucharistic spirituality, you must foster three essential habits: daily Mass, adoration of the Eucharist, and living the Mass. Each of these habits will cultivate an ever-growing eucharistic devotion and sustain you in your daily life.

Daily Mass is vital in the life of every seminarian and priest. Listening to the proclamation of the Word of God and receiving the Lord daily in Holy Communion are essential habits that must be continually strengthened in your life. As you commune with the Lord, your friendship with Him deepens. He communicates the love of His heart to you as

He touches and transforms your heart, and you grow in your love for Him. Fostering the following interior dispositions will help you experience the power of devoutly receiving Our Lord daily in Holy Communion. One disposition is to ask Our Lady to help you receive Christ as she received Him, with a pure and perfect love. You can pray, "My mother, help me to receive your Son as you received Him: with purity, humility, love, and devotion." Also, as you attend daily Mass, offer yourself in union with the sacrifice of the priest. Say in your heart, "Lord, I offer myself in union with this sacrifice." This habit is important because as a priest, when you are offering the Mass, your heart will already be disposed to offering yourself in union with the sacrifice of Jesus. This habit is also important because the Mass is the perfect place to offer our daily joys and sorrows to the Lord. The habit of daily Mass must remain strong even during summer recess. We tend to become lazy when we are not in our usual daily rhythm. Daily Mass will help you stay focused and disciplined in the spiritual life.

Second, do your best to spend time in eucharistic adoration, abiding with the Lord Jesus and listening to Him speak to you. A daily holy hour in the presence of the Lord is ideal. Just as Peter, James, and John saw Christ transfigured on Tabor, so each time you go before the Eucharist, you are with the same glorified Christ. Just as Moses' face glowed after he spoke to the Lord face-to-face, so you are transformed whenever you spend time before the eucharistic Lord. No time is wasted when you are in prayer before the Eucharist. As you spend time in adoration, you will find your love for Christ growing—precisely because you will come to know

His intimate, personal love for you. Do not worry about words as you adore Him: just be present to the Presence. I highly encourage you to spend time daily in the presence of the Eucharist. As a seminarian, growing in intimacy with Jesus enables your celibate heart to expand in love.

Finally, live the Mass. When the Mass ends, we are dismissed with the words, "Go in peace to love and to serve the Lord." We are commissioned to live the Love we have received. The Eucharist is the sacrament of charity. Go forth from the Mass to live the Eucharist. In word and deed, be Christ's living image to others. See Christ in others, and allow them see Him in you. You are His living tabernacle. St. Josemaria Escriva spent his entire day in thanksgiving for the Mass, and then in the evening, he would begin his interior preparation for Mass the next day. He knew how to live the Mass, and we do well to imitate him.

Love the Eucharist, and live the Eucharist. If you make the Eucharist the center of your life, you can be sure that your vocation will be established on a strong foundation.

With prayer before the Eucharist for you,

Father Najim

Questions for Prayer

"I exist for the Eucharist." What stirs in my heart as I consider this statement?

How can I live the Eucharist in my daily life?

The thoughts, feelings, and desires that surfaced as I read this letter:

My prayer:

True Devotion to Mary

"Behold, I am the handmaid of the Lord.
May it be done to me according to your word."
Lk. 1:38

My Dear Brother,

Let me share with you how my devotion to Mary began. I traveled to Medjugorje for the first time in May of 1990. I was sixteen. In 1981, six young people related that Mary appeared to them on a hillside; and from that day, she has continued to appear, giving messages of prayer, fasting, and conversion. My late grandmother, one of the holiest women I have ever known, invited me to go there with her on a pilgrimage. Since I was young and not very enthusiastic about my faith at the time, I did not know what to expect.

When my grandmother and I arrived in the small Bosnian town, we walked to the local Church of St. James with others in our group. I vividly remember standing in front of Our Lady's statue in the courtyard in front of the Church. With one hand on her heart and her other arm outstretched, it seemed as though Mary, in this statue, was asking me to take her hand. In my heart, I did take her hand; and I keep holding on to her hand, though there are days when I fail miserably. Whatever the final ruling of the Church is on the authenticity of these apparitions, I will always believe that the Lord used my trip to Medjugorje to bring me closer to His Mother and, ultimately, to Him.

True devotion to Mary is the fruit of authentic growth in holiness. *Totus Tuus*, "Totally Yours," the episcopal motto of Pope John Paul II, expresses the interior reality he lived throughout his life, his own true devotion to Mary. We, too, should take his words as our motto and live the mystery it implies. We should belong completely to Mary. But what does it mean to belong to Mary? It means entrusting ourselves to her every day, consecrating our life and vocation to her, knowing that she will take care of us. It means letting her form us just as she formed Jesus; and as she forms us, her virtues come to life in us. Some may not completely understand this idea of "belonging to Mary." To me, it seems so logical. Think about it: by belonging to Mary, are we not imitating Christ, who literally belonged to her?

Your relationship with the Blessed Virgin Mary is one of the most important aspects of your spiritual life, your life as a true man of God. Devotion to Mary cannot be seen as an option for you; fostering a relationship with Mary is essential to your growth in holiness. While you are in the seminary, and throughout your life as a priest, you must allow yourself to be formed by her, just as Christ was formed by her. The heart of Marian devotion is this: just as Christ entrusted Himself to Mary—He literally entered into her womb—we imitate Him by entrusting ourselves to her. As Christ was formed by her love, we offer ourselves to her to be formed by her love. Devotion to Mary has one goal: union with Jesus Christ.

If you have not yet formed the habit of praying the rosary, I encourage you to do so. The rosary, rather than being a mindless, repetitious prayer, is a profoundly contemplative prayer. Pope John Paul II described the rosary as contemplating Jesus with Mary, entering into the school of Mary. When we pray the rosary and allow Mary to form us, we begin to see with her eyes. And who better to teach us how to contemplate Jesus than she who contemplated Him daily? When we pray the rosary, we are conformed more deeply to the mysteries of Christ's life. When we pray the rosary, the dispositions of Mary's heart become our own. As the rosary becomes a regular part of our spiritual lives, we begin to understand the meaning of St. Paul's words, "I live, no longer I, but Christ lives in me" (Gal. 2:20).

Another sign of our devotion to Mary is the scapular. A scapular is an exterior sign of an interior reality: our consecration to her. Each morning, when I place my scapular around my neck, I say a very simple prayer: *Mary, clothe me in your virtues.* By living in union with Mary, she begins to form us in her virtues. Besides the cardinal and theological virtues, which Mary perfectly possessed, tradition teaches about ten virtues that we should strive to imitate from her life: purity, prudence, humility, faith, devotion, obedience, poverty, patience, mercy, and sorrow (in our case, sorrow for our sins, but also for the sins of the world). Each of these virtues should be alive in the heart of every seminarian and priest. Loving the Mother of God is the best way to grow in these virtues.

The simple truth is that when we grow in our love and devotion to Mary, we are interiorly drawn to surrender our lives to her Son; in fact, she invites us *into her surrender.* This is what it means to be formed by her. "May it be done to me according to your word" (Lk. 1:38): Mary's life is summarized in that one line. She is inviting us to share in her disposition, her interior life, which was always a "Yes" to the Lord. You see, when Mary said "Yes" to the angel, she conceived Christ in her womb. When we say "Yes" to the Lord—when we say: *Yes, Lord, I will pray; yes, Lord, I will love; yes, Lord, I will sacrifice; yes, Lord, I will forgive; yes, Lord, I will adore you in the Eucharist; yes, Lord, I will go to frequent confession; yes, Lord, I will pray the rosary; yes, Lord, I will obey and love the Church; yes, Lord, I will even suffer—* when we say "Yes" to Him, we conceive Christ in our hearts. Just as Mary physically gave birth to Christ, we make Jesus present in the world by living God's will in our daily lives—our daily "Yes."

The prayer of Mary, "*May it be done to me,*" (Lk. 1:38) must be our prayer. *Lord, I am yours; do with me what you will; whatever you want me to do, I will do; wherever you want me to go, I will go.* Each day, we can pray the words of St. Ignatius' *Suscipe*, which are truly Marian in character: *Take, Lord, and receive all my liberty, my memory, my understanding, my will, all that I have and possess. You have given everything to me; to you do I return it. All is yours, dispose of it according to your will. Give me only your love and your grace, for these are enough for me.*

With prayer to Our Lady for you,

Father Najim

69

Questions for Prayer

Do I see devotion to Mary as an option or as essential to becoming a holy priest?

How can I grow in my devotion to Mary and live that devotion on a daily basis?

The thoughts, feelings, and desires that surfaced as I read this letter:

My prayer:

The Father's Love

"Whoever is without love does not know God, for God is love."
1 Jn. 4:8

My Dear Brother,

If you are going to be an effective priest, you must know the love of God. I am not just talking about knowing how to explain God's love theologically; many can do that. I am talking about knowing the passionate, personal love of God the Father—experientially—in your daily life. You must know the love our Lord has for you *personally*. I challenge you to be honest with yourself: Have you experienced His love for you? Have you allowed your heart to be touched and transformed by His love?

You see, as a priest you will be the living presence of Jesus Christ to God's people. If you do not know the love that the Father has for you personally, then you will not be able to communicate His love to your people. If you do not know the love He has for you, then how will you be able to lead people into the loving embrace of Christ? Time and again, I have seen zealous seminarians and priests who try to preach the truths of the faith but ultimately end up turning people off. True, they give the content of the Church's teaching, but they explain the faith legalistically, coldly, even harshly. I wonder if they have allowed themselves to be touched deeply by the Father's love. Orthodoxy without

71

love is like Ezekiel's vision of the dry bones: there is no heart or flesh.

Jesus was deeply aware in His heart of His identity: He is the beloved Son of the Father. Christ invites you and me into that same reality. You and I are beloved sons of the Father. But it is not enough to know this truth intellectually; we must have a deep, abiding, heartfelt awareness that we are beloved sons. Our sonship is our deepest identity. Have you let the Father love you and reveal to you that you are indeed His beloved son?

For people to commit their lives to the Lord and embrace the teachings of the Church, they must be invited to know His love in their hearts. When people truly know the life-transforming love of God, then it is easier for them to embrace the truth. You are the one called to lead people into the loving embrace of the Father; but you cannot do that *if you do not live in His embrace.* This is why knowing His love for you and reflecting on His love daily is so important.

How can you come to experience God's love for you? Only through prayer can you know the love of God in your heart. You must ponder His love and allow Him to touch and transform you. Do you open your heart to Him in prayer and ask Him to reveal His love to you? Do you meditate upon the crucified Christ, realizing that He loved you personally on the cross and is now inviting you into the Father's heart? Have you acknowledged before the Lord the obstacles to His love that exist in your heart—feelings of unworthiness, lack of love for yourself, relationships that have left you scarred, patterns of sin that block His love?

My brother, you and I are in need of healing. Let us not fool ourselves. Bare your soul to God the Father!

At the end of each day, sit in silence in the presence of our Lord. Beg Him to give you the grace of His Holy Spirit, and ask yourself: *Where did I experience God's love today? In what moments did I experience His love and presence most intensely? Who did I encounter today that revealed God's love to me? How did I reveal God's love to others today?* When you ask yourself these or similar questions, you will begin to experience His presence in your heart in a powerful way. If you do this daily, you will be more deeply aware of His love and presence in your daily life. When you become more deeply aware of God's love and presence in your daily life, you will be less inclined to give in to unhealthy self-love. Another question to ask in His presence: *Where did I give in selfishness today?* When we are honest with ourselves, we will see that we give in to selfishness every day. But the more we meditate on the experiences of the Father's love in our daily lives, the more He will purify us of selfishness.

Yes, my brother, you must be in touch with your heart and the presence of the Father therein. The hearts of the saints burned with the love of God; that love drove them daily. You and I must know His love so that we, in turn, can reveal His love to His people who long to know Him.

Take a few moments now, and open yourself to receive His love for you.

With prayer for knowing God's love,

Father Najim

Questions for Prayer

In what ways have I experienced the Father's personal love for me?

Am I deeply aware of my identity as a beloved son of the Father? If not, who can help me become more deeply aware of this reality?

The thoughts, feelings, and desires that surfaced as I read this letter:

My prayer:

The Daily Examen and Fruits of the Holy Spirit

"The fruit of the Spirit is love, joy, peace, patience, kindness, generosity, faithfulness, self-control."
Gal. 5:22-23

My Dear Brother,

Perhaps, by now, the newness of the seminary has worn off, and you have hit a rut, feeling burdened by the daily routine. This is a great grace, for now you have an opportunity to grow in perseverance and to take a closer look at the action of the Holy Spirit and how you are responding to God's love in your daily life.

Once again, St. Ignatius can be our tutor here. In his *Spiritual Exercises*, he writes about the experience of spiritual consolation and spiritual desolation (especially Week 1, Rules 3 and 4). All of us experience those feelings almost every day. Have you ever noticed that we vacillate throughout the day? At one moment we can be in prayer in the chapel in great peace; the next moment, we may encounter someone who really gets on our nerves and we become aggravated. On Tuesday morning, we may be ministering to someone in need and experience interior joy; on Tuesday afternoon, studying for an exam, we find ourselves miserable. A friend calls us on the phone, interrupting work on a major project, but we are patient because he needs us; later we hit a traffic jam on the way to field education and are on the verge of road rage. One day, we wake up refreshed and filled with energy for life; the next day, we would rather stay in bed until noon. Yes, we vacillate—sometimes dramatically. At times, these daily mood swings can deeply affect us on the spiritual level if we are not deeply rooted in the Lord.

St. Ignatius wants us to understand that underneath all of the vacillating is the deeper reality of the virtues of faith, hope, and love—the deeper reality of God's loving presence in and around us. In his book *The Discernment of Spirits,* Father Timothy Gallagher writes about how non-spiritual desolation can lead to deeper—and pernicious—spiritual desolation.[4] For example, the fatigue that leads you to stay in bed could lead to lethargy in your prayer and, thus, to feeling distant from the Lord. So, in order to be unmoved by these daily fluctuations, our hearts must be deeply rooted in an unwavering awareness of God's passionate love for us. Each moment in our daily lives is an opportunity for us to be more deeply aware of God's love, to surrender to His love for us, to fall more deeply in love with Him.

One of my favorite passages is St. Paul's description of the fruits of the Holy Spirit. He tells the Galatians that "the fruit of the Spirit is love, joy, peace, patience, kindness, generosity, faithfulness, gentleness, self-control" (5:22-23). Instead of wanting us to be controlled by the frequent vacillations of our daily life, the Lord desires that the fruits of the Spirit be fully alive in us. If we develop a deep heart-knowledge of God's loving presence in our lives, then the fruits of the Holy Spirit will grow in us; and the pull of the flesh and daily vacillations will not weigh us down.

How do you avail yourself more completely to the action of the Holy Spirit in your life? St. Ignatius recommended a method of daily prayer that will help you not only to grow in the fruits of the Spirit, but also to aid you in becoming more deeply aware of and receptive to God's love, as well as the way in which you resist the movements of the Holy Spirit. As we become more able to recognize the movements away from the fruits of the Holy Spirit, we are more able to reject them and to turn to the Lord.

St. Ignatius proposed the daily examen. You have, no doubt, heard about—and probably even practice—the examination of conscience. In this we meditate upon our sins and move toward repentance. In the examen, we become aware of God's presence, love, and action in our lives. He wanted his followers to be aware of the Lord's love and grace as the foundation of their lives and so receive these more deeply each day. For this reason, he would not dispense his followers from praying the daily examen. To this day, Jesuits are required to pray the examen twice a day for fifteen minutes.

How does one go about praying the daily examen? St. Ignatius proposed the following:

- *Transition.* As you begin the examen, take a few moments to become aware of the love with which God looks upon you. Silence yourself to be aware of His love.

- *Step One: Gratitude.* Take some time to note the gifts that God has given you today, and give thanks to God for them. These gifts are concrete signs of God's love for you.

- *Step Two*: *Petition*. Ask the Lord for an insight and a strength that will make this examen a work of grace, fruitful beyond your human capacity. Pray with the words that the Holy Spirit inspires in you.

- *Step Three*: *Review*. With the Lord, review your day. Reflect on where you are responding to God's indwelling love and where you have said *yes* or *no* to permitting Him to love you more. Look for the stirrings in your heart and the thoughts, feelings, and desires that God has given you today. Also look for those thoughts that have not been of God. Review your choices in response to both categories.

- *Step Four*: *Forgiveness*. Ask for the healing touch and embrace of the forgiving God, who removes your heart's burdens.

- *Step Five*: *Renewal*. Look to the following day, and, with God, make choices in your heart to accept the interior movements of the Spirit that speak to you of His love, and reject in faith those interior movements that are selfish or desolating.

- *Transition*: Aware of God's loving presence with you and aware of God loving you, prayerfully conclude the examen with a faith-filled *yes* to trusting in God's desire to lead and guide you.[5]

As you can see, the examen is far more than acknowledging what we have done wrong; the examen assists us in becoming deeply aware of God's loving presence and action in our daily lives. Becoming more sensitive to the consolations and desolations we experience throughout the day is the heart of the examen, and it opens us to the Spirit's invitation to fall more in love with Him. The wisdom in praying the daily examen is that it keeps us rooted in God's presence and enables us to be more contemplative throughout the day. Remember, the Holy Trinity dwells in us. Jesus speaks in and through consolations when we are sincerely seeking His presence in our lives. The examen also fortifies us against the radical vacillations we experience on a daily basis. Certainly, we will still experience these fluctuations; but as we become more deeply aware of God's loving presence and action in our lives, we will remain steadfast in the Lord against such temptations.

Another good practice, in addition to the examen, is to memorize the fruits of the Holy Spirit so that you can check yourself against them during the day or at the end of the day as a quick way to see if you are remaining attentive to God's loving presence during the day. Take a few minutes and review the fruits by asking yourself: Today, have I been loving, joyful, peaceful, patient, kind, generous, faithful, gentle, and chaste? To remind myself to review the fruits of the Holy Spirit, I have an electronic calendar that lists a different fruit each day.

By praying the daily examen and focusing on the fruits of the Holy Spirit, you will be much less likely to be overwhelmed each time you are tempted to give in to desolation. You will be aware of God's indwelling presence and the fruits of the Holy Spirit rather than the fruits of the self-centered desires of the flesh. You will also experience a deep interior transformation which will lead to a flourishing of the fruits of the Holy Spirit in your life. When you pray the daily examen, you become more aware of how you respond to God's love in your daily life. The fruits of the Spirit will continue to grow in you, and your heart will be filled more and more with the Lord's loving presence so that you will rejoice in His loving presence more and more. Even when you are sad or simply downcast, God wants you to know His love. Resist allowing these simple, negative emotions to descend into a state of feeling separated from God's love. God will help you to know you are always His beloved son.

With prayer in our daily examen,

Father Najim

Questions for Prayer

Am I governed by the daily vacillations of my life or by the fruits of the Holy Spirit?

What effects might I experience in my life if I began to incorporate the daily examen into my prayer?

The thoughts, feelings, and desires that surfaced as I read this letter:

My prayer:

The Cross

"Now I rejoice in my sufferings..."
Col. 1:24

My Dear Brother,

Will you be surprised if you experience trials that cause interior turmoil in your heart? Tell me, since you are on the path to priesthood, to be another Christ, do you honestly think you will not encounter the cross? Did you think it will be a smooth road? As you strive to grow daily in union with Christ, do you expect Him to lead you to walk with Him everywhere except to Calvary? If we seek union with Jesus, then we must know that He will unite us with every mystery of His life—not just the joyful, glorious, and luminous mysteries, but the sorrowful as well. He wants to live His holy mysteries in and through us.

What you must do here is exactly what Our Lord did. He embraced the cross with love; He did not do it grudgingly. Do you not believe that Jesus knows what you are experiencing? Do you not believe that He knew, from all eternity, that you would be experiencing these interior struggles? Do you not believe that, in a mysterious way, He is allowing this struggle for your sanctification and the sanctification of those whom you will soon serve? You must do exactly what He did: cry out to Him in weakness as He cried out to the Father so that you can receive the strength that He received from the Father.

I recall a time when I was going through a difficult time in the seminary. My experience was dark and confusing; my mind was filled with vocational doubts, and I could not understand why the Lord was allowing such thoughts. Because it was a time of desolation, the temptation to doubt and question the Lord was always present. But that challenging experience drove me to my knees more than any other time in seminary. I remember how sincerely I sought the Lord in prayer and how open I was with my spiritual director. Each time I prayed the Way of the Cross in the chapel, I was consoled. Each time I prayed the Way of the Cross, I experienced a nearness to Christ that eased the weight of my burden. Those experiences were not coincidental. *I prayerfully related my sorrow to His sorrow, and I received what He received: consolation from the Father.*

I still do not completely understand why the Lord allowed me to go through that trial, but I do know the valuable spiritual lesson He taught me. Experiencing the cross in our lives is an invitation to unite ourselves with Christ in His suffering. Being in the midst of trial is an invitation from the Lord to grow in friendship with Him. It requires a change of thinking on our part: That you are suffering means Jesus knows you are ready to enter into His life in a deeper way; that you are suffering means Jesus loves you so much that He wants you to share in His cross and experience the depth of His love for you. Suffering, ultimately, is a profound and life-transforming grace.

Remember, at the heart of every priest's life is the call to sacrifice. Jesus, our Eternal High Priest, offered the ultimate sacrifice for our salvation. When experiencing difficulties in your life, develop the habit of uniting yourself and your trial with the sacrifice of the priest at Mass. By doing this, you are uniting your trial with the perfect sacrifice, and your suffering becomes redemptive. When you are a priest, you will be able to offer your sufferings to the Lord as *you* celebrate the Mass, and this, too, is a wonderful imitation of our Lord. He offered Himself for our salvation; we can offer ourselves in union with Him for the salvation of the people whom we serve.

My brother, each trial you experience is a wonderful opportunity for growth. You need to understand that God loves you in your weakness, in your poverty, in your brokenness. In fact, we encounter Him most deeply in our weakness. Do you believe He loves you in your weakness, in your brokenness? Do not be afraid to be weak before Him, to open your heart so that He may enter into your weakness and brokenness. Cry out to the Lord in weakness. He wants to embrace you where you are.

On retreat several years ago, I read the biography of Terrence Cardinal Cooke. He was a man who experienced deep suffering in his life and understood that it was all grace. He kept a prayer card in his breviary with these words:

> *The everlasting God has in his wisdom foreseen from eternity the cross that he now presents to you as a gift from his inmost heart. This cross he now sends you he has considered with his all-knowing eyes, understood with his divine mind, tested with his wise justice, warmed with loving arms and weighed with his own hands to see that it be not one inch too large and not one ounce too heavy for you. He has blessed it*

with his holy Name, anointed it with his grace, perfumed it with his consolation, taken one last glance at you and your courage, and then sent it to you from Heaven, a special greeting to you, an alms of the all-merciful love of God.[6]

Reflect on these words, for they are spoken to you.

With prayer in suffering,

Father Najim

Questions for Prayer

How is Christ inviting me to share more deeply in His Passion?

"At the heart of every priest's life is the call to sacrifice." What can I do in my daily life to help me to grow in sacrificial love?

The thoughts, feelings, and desires that surfaced as I read this letter:

My prayer:

Spiritual Warfare

"So submit yourselves to God.
Resist the devil, and he will flee from you."
James 4:7

My Dear Brother,

In this letter, I desire to share with you a profound, though often ignored, truth of the spiritual life: we *are* in a war. St. Paul asserted, "For our struggle is not with flesh and blood but with the principalities, with the powers, with the world rulers of this present darkness, with the evil spirits in the heavens" (Eph. 6:12). Yes, my brother, you must know that since you are on the path to the priesthood, the devil will do his absolute best to make sport of you. He will be relentless in trying to dissuade you from pursuing your vocation to the priesthood.

Now, I do not say this to frighten you or to put undo focus on the evil one, but if you think for one moment that you are not a target of the devil, you are fooling yourself. One of Satan's greatest tricks is to try to make us forget about him. When we forget about him and his attacks, we become less vigilant in guarding ourselves against him. Each and every day, we must invoke the protection of our Lord, Our Lady, and our guardian angels. I have a particular fondness for my namesake, St. Michael. He does, in truth, defend us in battle.

The devil will try to make you stumble and then to keep you down. One of his favorite tactics is kicking us when we are down. Most of us have experienced this. We are progressing steadily in the spiritual life; our relationship with the Lord is strong, and then ... BAM! We fall, and we feel like it is the ultimate fall. Then, the devil begins to blackmail us. His voice is subtle but very real: *See, you are too weak to be a priest; you are unable to do it; you will continue to fail. Feel the shame of this moment; wallow in your shame; loathe yourself. God is disappointed in you. Do not go to Him in prayer. You ought to just leave the seminary; you know you will be happier without having to strive so hard. Pack your bags; a better world is out there waiting for you.*

St. Josemaría Escrivá cautioned us to be on guard against this temptation of the devil. He wrote: "Do you hear these words? 'In another state in life, in another place, in another position or occupation, you would do much more good. Talent isn't needed for what you are doing.' Well, listen to me: Wherever you have been placed, you please God..., and what you've just been thinking is clearly a suggestion of the devil."[7]

How can we overcome the daily temptations that we experience? How can we win this daily spiritual battle? First and foremost, we must acknowledge that we cannot win the battle solely on our own power. If we try to fight by ourselves, we are sure to lose. The way to win is to surrender. That sounds like a paradox, but it is a sure path to victory in the spiritual life.

By humbly surrendering ourselves to the Lord *at the beginning* of temptation, we allow His power to reign in us.

Read what St. James teaches us about resistance: "So submit yourselves to God. Resist the devil, and he will flee from you. Draw near to God, and he will draw near to you" (James 4:7-8). Notice that he tells us first to submit to God and *then* resist. Why? Precisely in submitting to God, we receive the power to resist. St. Paul attests to this truth, recounting the words our Lord spoke to him: "My grace is sufficient for you, for *power is made perfect in weakness*" (2 Cor. 12:9; emphasis added).

My brother, temptation is an opportunity for us to allow God to strengthen our wills; put more directly, resisting temptation is an opportunity to grow in virtue. A priest whom I know used this analogy: if we were being physically attacked, we would naturally defend ourselves; we would fight back. The same should be true in the spiritual life. My friend said we need to be like spiritual ninjas. We need to fight back. But we do not fight back by taking on the temptation of the devil directly. In the moment of temptation, we must stand firm in the Lord and submit to Him—that is how we fight back; that is how we win. We cannot be afraid or think it odd to get on our knees in the moment of temptation. We must reject timidity. In fact, a fitting tactic in these moments is to say out loud and with authority: *I belong to Jesus Christ! I surrender to you, Lord. In the name of Jesus Christ, I command you to be gone, Satan!* Waiting too long to ask for help makes the resistance that much more unlikely. Develop the habit of submitting to God and resisting at the beginning of temptation, thus making your heart grow stronger.

Remember, also, the means that the Lord has given to the Church to help us in battle. Some people may try to persuade you to believe that the use of holy water, sacramentals, and devotion to your guardian angel is immature pietism. Do not believe them. What they call "immature pietism," I call weapons for the battle, and so does the Church.

Speaking of weapons for the battle, St. Paul tells us what we need to be well equipped: "Finally, draw your strength from the Lord and from his mighty power. Put on the armor of God so that you may be able to stand firm against the tactics of the devil.... So stand fast with your loins girded in truth, clothed with righteousness as a breastplate, and your feet shod in readiness for the gospel of peace. In all circumstances, hold faith as a shield, to quench all (the) flaming arrows of the evil one. And take the helmet of salvation and the sword of the Spirit, which is the word of God" (Eph. 6:10-11, 14-17).

Yes, we are targets of the devil, but more importantly, we are objects of the love and grace of God. We must remember that we are victorious in Christ. Jesus overcame the devil when He was in the desert; and in overcoming the devil's temptations, He merited for us the grace to do the same. St. Augustine reminds us of Christ's victory over Satan: "If in Christ we have been tempted, in him we overcome the devil. Do you think only of Christ's temptations and fail to think of his victory? See yourself as tempted in him, and see yourself as victorious in him. He could have kept the devil from himself; but if he were not tempted he could not teach you how to triumph over temptation."[8]

Yes, my brother, we are born into a world at war. And this war wages on. You are called to be a warrior in the battle. The more seriously you take the call to holiness, the more the devil will try to bring you down. But you need not fear; remain aware and be on guard. In the midst of temptation, let your heart be strengthened in Christ. Draw all your strength from communion with Christ!

With prayer for the battle,

Father Najim

Questions for Prayer

What tactics of the devil am I most susceptible to, and how can I fight against them?

"You are called to be a warrior in the battle." What does this thought stir in my heart?

The thoughts, feelings, and desires that surfaced as I read this letter:

My prayer:

Chaste Celibacy

*"Some are incapable of marriage ... because they have
renounced marriage for the sake of the kingdom of heaven."*
Mt. 19:12

My Dear Brother,

I knew at some point that writing these letters would
require me to share my thoughts about celibacy. But where
do I begin? So much can be said about this most beautiful,
yet very misunderstood, gift that Christ has entrusted to the
Church. I say that celibacy is misunderstood because the av-
erage person, even many Catholics, "just don't get it"; they
cannot understand why a healthy man or woman would
commit to a life without marital intimacy. When most people hear the word *celibacy*, they think: *no sex.* They see nothing positive about celibacy; all they see is sacrifice. Please,
make sure that is not *your* view of celibacy. For us, celibacy
is not so much about giving something up but about giving
something—giving *ourselves*—away in love.

When I preach on the subject of the priesthood, I
always speak about the gift of celibate love. Yes, celibate *love.*
My hope is to help parishioners understand that the Church
is enriched by celibacy. Just as marriage and family life is a
gift to the Church and is a revelation of God's self-giving
love, so, too, is celibacy a gift to the Church and a revelation of God's self-giving love. I explain that some people are
called to celibacy for the Kingdom of God; some are called
to follow Christ in the same way He was embodied.

The call to celibacy is an invitation from the Lord to love Him with an undivided heart, to make His sacrificial love present in the world, and to point people to heaven through the powerful sign value in remaining celibate for the Kingdom. Remember, marriage does not exist in heaven; in heaven, everyone is a chaste celibate. Therefore, those called to celibacy on earth are living reminders that our true home is heaven. Celibacy is a sign to the world that the deepest longing of the human heart is union with God.

I cannot emphasize this point enough: if you are called to the priesthood, then you are called to *love* celibately, not just to *live* celibately. And remember, by loving celibately, you are not giving up intimacy; you are opening yourself to deeper intimacy with the Lord and His people. Intimacy is another misunderstood concept. Physical intimacy does not necessarily result in true intimacy. Sadly, the opposite is often true: physical intimacy, whenever separated from its true meaning and purpose, leads to isolation and loneliness. A well-integrated celibate understands that intimacy is not solely physical. The priest who loves celibately experiences an expansion of his heart and profound intimacy, not isolation and loneliness.

If a priest is loving celibately and not simply living celibately, he will be deeply aware of moments of intimacy in his life: At the end of a long day when he is exhausted from ministry, he will experience intimacy as he opens his heart in prayer and allows the Lord to comfort him. Sitting in the confessional on a Saturday afternoon, he will experience intimacy as a penitent weeps in sorrow for her sins. On a Sunday morning, as he is celebrating Mass, he will experience intimacy as he looks out on the congregation and sees a parishioner who only he knows is suffering. As he is called out in the middle of the night to a nearby hospital, he will experience intimacy as he anoints a person who will soon die and as he spends time with a grieving family.

As a man being called to chaste, celibate love, you must have this capacity for intimacy. The only way this capacity for intimacy grows is by having a very deep, personal relationship with Jesus Christ. Each of us possesses a desire for intimacy; the desire for intimacy is a holy desire. At its root, it is a desire for God. Speak your desire for intimacy to the Lord. Do not be afraid to bring your sexual desires to Him in prayer. You need not be ashamed of your sexual passions. Be completely transparent before the Lord. Ultimately, when purified, the sexual urge is a desire for loving union. Nothing is more beautiful than bringing these desires to the Lord so that He can unite us more deeply with His passionate, loving heart.

So often, young people ask me if I wish I had a wife and children of my own. I always tell them that these thoughts sometimes pass through my mind. All priests will have these moments. But they are certainly not persistent, daily thoughts; in fact, these thoughts are very rare. I always explain that I am wed to the Church. The priest is called to be a chaste spouse of the Church. Priests are called to spiritual fatherhood, and the way to live this spiritual fatherhood is by living celibacy joyfully, passionately, and generously. If a priest is living his spiritual fatherhood and his spousal relationship with the Church, he will experience deep peace and fulfillment in his life.

Spiritual fatherhood, chaste spousal union with the Church, intimacy with the Lord and His people, passionate love for Christ and His people, a full and joyful life—all these concepts describe the gift of celibacy. Celibacy is not about loneliness and empty sacrifice. Celibacy is about love. If you see only the sacrifice and not the gift, then you are missing the most important point.

With prayer for joyful celibacy,

Father Najim

Questions for Prayer

Do I experience celibacy more as a gift or as a sacrifice?

What are the ways in which I experience intimacy in my daily life?

The thoughts, feelings, and desires that surfaced as I read this letter:

My prayer:

Chaste Celibacy: How To Live It

"But you, be self-possessed in all circumstances."
2 Tim. 4:5

My Dear Brother,

Though I did not want to overwhelm you with too many thoughts on celibacy in my last letter, I desire to share some practical ways that help a priest to love celibately. Sacrifice is involved, and a priest must always maintain his boundaries. Remembering that the priest *freely chooses* to live chaste celibacy is important; he ought not to feel that it is imposed upon him. Thus, understanding the difference between simply accepting celibacy and embracing celibacy is vital. If a seminarian or priest simply *accepts* celibacy, or *endures* it, he will never be happy in the priesthood. He must interiorly embrace celibacy as the way that God has created him to love. The seminarian must form the interior habit of chaste celibacy, and to do this, he needs support. Let me share with you what I have found to be helpful in living chaste celibacy.

First and foremost, we must be men of prayer. In order for our celibate love to be fruitful, we must cultivate a deep interior life. Our prayer cannot be superficial; rather, it must be intimate, passionate, and intense. We must constantly desire union with Christ and allow the Holy Spirit to form continually in us the habit of surrendering our minds, hearts, and bodies to Christ. Similar to what I wrote concerning prayer, we must learn to live in the embrace of Christ and to be comfortable there. "I love you, Jesus," is a daily prayer that ought to flow easily from our hearts and lips. We must listen to Jesus speaking His love to us. Do not be afraid to bring your whole being to prayer: your heart, mind, and passions. As I wrote in my last letter, you can also become comfortable bringing your sexuality and any sexual issues to the Lord in prayer as you experience His desire to embrace you and encourage you.

The second support is regular spiritual direction. Spiritual direction is one of the most important aspects of seminary formation—and priesthood, as well. Honesty in direction, especially regarding chaste, celibate living, is vital. You should be willing to speak with your director about your growth in chaste celibacy, as well as about your struggles, not fearing the dark areas of your life but, rather, bringing them to the light. You can become comfortable talking to your director about your sexuality and any struggles you are having, as well as sharing with him the positive aspects of your growth in understanding and living chaste celibacy. Hiding your struggles from your director is very unhealthy and will lead to affective problems in the future. Spiritual and affective transparency in spiritual direction are crucial to developing the virtue of chastity. Do not be afraid to reveal the truth to God and to your director.

The third support is frequent confession. As you know, the Sacrament of Reconciliation is one of the great helps that we, Catholics, have in our lives. With regard to chaste celibacy, confession keeps us honest with ourselves and with the Lord. Confession gives us the grace to grow in holiness, and the grace to keep up the struggle. As with spiritual direction, confession helps us to bring to the light the things that we would rather keep in the darkness.

The fourth support is having good spiritual friendships with other seminarians so that you can talk about the joys and struggles of living chaste celibacy. Having a couple of seminarian or priest friends in whom you can confide is important and provides another opportunity to bring your struggles into the light. After all, Jesus surrounded Himself with the apostles. Your circle of friends should not be limited to seminarians and priests, however. Good and warm relationships with family members and other friends is also healthy and important.

The fifth support is keeping proper boundaries in relationships. Yes, developing friendships with both men and women is valuable, but it is also important for you to keep proper boundaries in these relationships, especially those with women. You must be honest with yourself, and ask yourself these questions: *Is there any person to whom I am particularly attracted? What are my feelings? Am I flirtatious? Do I send the wrong signals in any relationship?* We should not be cold and distant in our relationships, but we need to have a deep self-awareness of what we are experiencing toward people in our lives and to learn to sense flirtations from others, too.

The sixth support is maintaining a sense of humor. This might sound strange, but it is true. Cultivating the spirit of joy is indispensable; and while we need to take life seriously, we must also be lighthearted about ourselves. Take your struggles seriously, but be able to laugh through them. Here is an example: Let us say that you are at the mall using the gift card you received at Christmas to buy a new shirt and pants, and you find the sales clerk very attractive. After you leave the store, you can berate yourself for taking a second glance, or you can laugh at yourself for being weak. Believe me, the second option is much better and healthier. By keeping a sense of humor, you will avoid being overcome by your weaknesses, and your struggles will actually have less of a hold on you.

The seventh support is love of solitude. In order for us to have a rich interior life, we must develop a love for solitude. When we are in silence and alone with God, we can more easily cultivate intimacy with Him. Intimacy with the Lord is necessary for us to live a chaste, celibate life. Intimacy with the Lord expands the heart and our capacity for intimacy with others. Solitude is paradoxical: we desire *to be alone* only so that we might be *more available for communion with God.* Solitude serves our desire to deepen our love for God through a lively, dynamic interior life.

The eighth support is appreciating the good in the culture. To live chaste celibacy, it is helpful to develop a love for good music, theater, art, good books, movies, and other positive cultural experiences. These things lift the spirit and help us to experience transcendent love. Since paying attention to such beauty purifies the conscience and strengthens the will, we are then better able to resist the lower inclinations of our nature. To be habitually inclined to the beautiful creates within us an affective dissatisfaction with all grossly sinful artistic expressions. We learn, instead, that God calls to us from within the beautiful and we begin to seek out cultural expressions that clearly carry that call.

The ninth support is staying physically healthy. What does this mean on a practical level? It means that you have to work your body. Get out and exercise: Take a brisk walk three or four days a week for thirty to forty-five minutes; start jogging; go swimming a few days a week; find an elliptical machine or a treadmill you can use; lift weights. Do something at least three or four days a week that will benefit your body and expend energy. Establish an exercise regimen that combines both cardiovascular and body-strengthening exercises. You will feel better about yourself because you will have more energy and focus, and you will grow in self-mastery. You also want to make sure you are maintaining a healthy diet. Avoid the high sugar and bad-fat foods that sap your energy. Taking care of yourself physically will benefit your growth in self-mastery, which in turn helps you live chastely.

In closing, let me offer a few more practical suggestions for living celibacy fully. Avoid the excessive use of alcohol, especially when you are alone. While alcohol in moderation is fine, it lowers our defenses and makes us vulnerable. Obviously, avoid places and establishments that are not conducive to chaste living; and avoid television channels, movies, music, and Web sites that tempt you to falter in valuing the virtue of chastity.

My brother, let the Lord be your all. Learn how Jesus' desire to love you is greater than your desire to love Him. As you bring Him your loneliness and your desire for children, which you will experience, His celibate love will be poured into your heart. Then, you can learn how He makes it possible for you to live His life. Be honest and open with yourself and your spiritual director. Do not hide your struggles. We all struggle, but the Lord has given us the support that we need to live a healthy, chaste, celibate life.

With prayer for living celibately,

Father Najim

Questions for Prayer

How have I interiorly embraced celibacy as a good?

Which supports for celibacy am I living well, and which supports do I need to cultivate?

The thoughts, feelings, and desires that surfaced as I read this letter:

My prayer:

Joyful Obedience

"He humbled himself, becoming obedient to death,
even death on a cross."
Phil. 2:8

My Dear Brother,

A seminarian once asked me: "Is it true that the promise of obedience is more difficult to live than the promise of celibacy?" This is a good question. Before I was ordained, I remember many priests telling me that obedience was the most difficult promise to live. First, each promise—celibacy, obedience, and prayer—has both joys and challenges; however, the man who possesses a deep understanding of his vocation to the priesthood and is living it to the fullest will experience many more blessings than struggles. My brother, you should already be able to answer this question about the promise of obedience. What do I mean? Well, are you not already living these promises? True, you have not officially promised celibacy, prayer, and obedience; but you are certainly living those promises now. Most seminarians would agree that they are living prayer and celibacy; many, however, may not consider obedience a daily part of their lives.

Just as you are living prayer and celibacy every day, you are also—at least you ought to be—living obedience every day because obedience is, first and foremost, *an interior reality*. I think many seminarians—and maybe even some priests—think of obedience simply as an external act. They make the mistake of limiting obedience to certain instances of submitting to authority: The bishop tells a priest to move, and he moves. The problem with this attitude is that it can lead to obedience becoming dormant in the heart. If obedience is not lived every day, just like prayer and celibacy, then it will be more difficult for the priest to be joyful in his obedience; in fact, he may even become angry when he is asked to manifest it externally. Obedience is much deeper than an external act. Obedience, in the truest sense, is an interior, daily surrender of the heart to the will of God, to the voice of the Good Shepherd speaking within you. As Jesus said, "the sheep hear his voice" (Jn. 10:3).

Yes, a man who is ordained a priest promises obedience to his bishop; but on a daily basis, he must be obedient to the voice of the Lord, to the promptings of the Holy Spirit in his heart. Your bishop will not ask you to take on a new assignment every day. The Lord, however, will ask something of you every day: to pray more, to sacrifice something, to reach out to someone else in need, to focus on living a particular fruit of the Holy Spirit. Every day, then, the question on your heart must be: *What are you asking of me today, Lord?*

To understand obedience in the deepest sense, we must contemplate Jesus in His obedience to the Father. The promise of obedience that you and I are called to live is rooted in Jesus' obedience to the will of His Father. As St. Paul tells us, Christ became "obedient to death, even death on a cross" (Phil. 2:8). The very reason you and I are capable of obedience to the Father—and to the Church—is that Christ first lived obedience in His humanity. The same is true for the promises of prayer and celibacy. The reason you and I are able to live these promises is because Christ lived them first. He gained for us the grace to live these promises, and to live them supernaturally and joyfully.

To live obedience joyfully, we must allow ourselves to be conformed to the will of Christ, who, in His humanity, was perfectly conformed to the will of the Father. How do we allow our wills to be conformed to Christ's will? Only through prayer. The saints teach us that it is most fruitful for us to contemplate Christ in His humanity, particularly in His passion. In order to grow in the virtue of obedience, I suggest that you contemplate Christ in the Garden of Gethsemane. "Father ... not my will but yours be done" (Lk. 22:42).

Remember, obedience is a daily promise; therefore, it ought to be a daily reality. Cultivate the habit of surrendering in obedience to the will of God every day. The question of the saints is, *What are you asking of me today, Lord?* As you ask this question, you will find within yourself a growing desire to embrace whatever He is asking of you.

Understanding and living the promise of obedience you made at ordination is possible only with this understanding of obedience. Before you make that promise, the interior virtue of obedience must be strong in your heart. If it is, you will be able to kneel before your bishop and promise not only obedience but *joyful* obedience.

When I was in seminary, and even in my early days as a priest, I used to say that the one assignment I absolutely did not want was to be the Vocation Director. Nothing appealed to me about being out of parish ministry; therefore, when the bishop asked me to go into vocation ministry, I was shocked, to say the least. I was extremely happy in my parish and had absolutely no desire to leave. When the bishop spoke to me about vocation ministry, he did not say, "I am assigning you to the seminary to work in vocation ministry." He said, "I am asking you *to consider* living at the seminary in order to do vocation ministry." "Can I speak to my spiritual director?" I asked. The bishop said, "Yes."

I sat down with my spiritual director and proposed my "dilemma" to him. I literally had written down on a piece of paper all the reasons I should stay at my parish and all the reasons I should leave. After all, the bishop had not *told* me that I *had* to go. When I was finished speaking, my spiritual director looked at me with perplexity and simply said, "But, Michael, the bishop asked you." That was it. I knew my answer, but it was a struggle to leave behind a place I loved so much. I knew in the depths of my heart that the Lord was asking me to move, but the initial decision was still difficult.

My brother, remember that your vocation to the priesthood is larger than you. Your priesthood is not about you but about service to the Lord and His Church. The obedience you promise is meant to serve the mission of the Church. God is wise. He may invite you to places you have never thought about or desired to go; but go, unhesitatingly and with joy. The good news of salvation will be furthered because of your obedience.

With prayer and obedience,

Father Najim

Questions for Prayer

How can I better live obedience to the Lord in my daily life?

Am I truly willing to do whatever the Lord and His Church ask me to do in my priesthood?

The thoughts, feelings, and desires that surfaced as I read this letter:

My prayer:

Simplicity of Life

"The Son of Man has nowhere to rest his head."
Lk. 9:58

My Dear Brother,

Living a simple life today may be much more difficult than it would have been in the past. Technology is a paradox: it has simultaneously made life more efficient and more difficult. Do not misunderstand me. Many modern technological advances are tremendous. Information that used to take hours to research is now just a click away. We can keep in touch daily with family and friends, even if they are thousands of miles away. The world is smaller today; however, as the world has shrunk, distractions have increased. We are bombarded with email, we receive instant messages as we are working, our cell phones ring, and we are getting text messages. As we work at our desks and at our computers, we can easily distract ourselves: *I'll just check to see tomorrow's weather forecast.* Neither the priest nor the seminarian is exempt from these distractions which have made it harder than ever before to live a simple life.

Technological distractions are not all that conspire against simplicity of life. If we understand that simplicity begins in the heart, in the interior life, then we can understand that if the heart is full of distractions, then those distractions will overflow to our exterior reality. To live a life of simplicity on the outside, we must live a life of simplicity on the inside. Our hearts must be fully alive in Christ. The more we are immersed in the life of God, who is perfectly simple, the more our capacity to live with simplicity will expand.

Priests are called to a life of simplicity. As a seminarian, you must begin to foster a simple life modeled on Christ's life. Simplicity of life can pose a particular challenge for the diocesan priest because he is not vowed to a life of poverty. He receives a salary, owns his own car, pays his own bills, buys his own clothes, and has his own financial investments. On any given day, he can go out and shop for a new computer, a new cell phone, a new car, or even new artwork for his living space. So how can a priest be *in* the world but not *of* the world?

First, simplicity of life means that a priest must be interiorly detached from the things of this world, even while possessing some of those things. In order to be interiorly detached, he must be interiorly *attached*—to God. In other words, a priest must desire Jesus Christ and Him alone. Only Christ can preserve the priest from becoming too worldly. Jesus Christ is our true wealth. He is all that we need. This essential truth must be deeply rooted in our hearts.

If we are not deeply attached to Christ, if we are not affectively united to Him, then inevitably, we will fall prey to filling our lives with worldly things, poor substitutes for a deep life in Christ. We will long for the newest technical gadget or the nicest car; filling our lives with distraction after distraction—hours online or hours in the mall, looking for that one item to buy that will entertain us until we tire of it. And then, we will look for the next best gadget. All the while, our hearts are longing for union with Jesus, but we cannot hear our deepest longing because we have become attached to things that just do not matter.

Not all material things are bad in themselves. Nothing is wrong with having money in the bank, a nicely decorated room, some nice clothes, a decent car, or a new cell phone. When we long for these things, when they take hold of our desires, when they become our focus or define who we are, we lose our simplicity. Jesus Christ desires to be the center of our lives. He and the mission He has entrusted to us must be our motivation.

Our lives need to be simple. The simpler our lives are, the more we are able to focus on the Lord and His call in our lives. Here I offer some practical ways to foster deeper simplicity in your life. Maintaining good order in your life—for example, keeping a clean room and an organized desk—can be very helpful. Focusing on such details might seem meticulous, but the axiom that the exterior reveals the interior is often true. If our exterior space is a mess, what does that say about our hearts? Personally, I hate clutter. A couple of times a year, I go through my rooms and eliminate things I do not need. I give away old clothes, get rid of unnecessary books, and clean my files. I find that when I do this, I have more clarity; I can work better, pray better, live better.

Another way to foster simplicity is by being generous with what we have, particularly with our money. Now, I know that as a seminarian, you probably do not have a lot of money to give away; however, giving to charity is still a good habit. When you are a priest, you should do your best to tithe. Giving to charity not only helps those who are less fortunate, but it also keeps us from becoming attached to what we have by maintaining awareness of those who have much less than we. Having a generous heart is also a true sign that the grace of Christ is active in your interior life, for He came to serve, not to be served.

Be careful not to overcomplicate your life or to cause scandal by the way you live. You will not need to buy a brand new Mercedes when you are a priest. You need a dependable car, but it does not need to be the finest. Will you really need a 60-inch, flat screen television in your room? Is purchasing a new cell phone every six months absolutely necessary? Do you have to check your email thirty-seven times a day, even while you are out to dinner with friends? Will you really need forty-five, non-clerical dress shirts? My brother, look at your life now, and make the changes necessary to live more simply. As priests, we really do not need a lot of material things.

Seminarians and priests are called to set an example of detachment. By the way we live, we should remind people that the most important part of our lives is a personal friendship with Jesus Christ. If we allow our lives to be filled with distractions, material or technological, then we will not be simple. And if we are not simple, it will be more difficult to pray. And if we do not pray, we will not be holy. And if we are not holy, then our lives become a tragedy. And—you get the point.

As with all things, make Christ your model. He certainly had a small wardrobe. He had no place to lay His head. He was poor. Yet, He is the Son of God, our Savior, the One to whom you have given your life. He is your wealth. He is all you need. Be simple, and it will be easier for you to be holy.

With prayer for simplicity,

Father Najim

Questions for Prayer

By the way I live, do people know that Christ is my wealth?

What do I need to do to live more simply?

The thoughts, feelings, and desires that surfaced as I read this letter:

My prayer:

Spiritual Fatherhood

"For I became your father in Christ Jesus through the gospel."
1 Cor. 4:15

My Dear Brother,

I remember it vividly. It was Father's Day. I had just celebrated Mass, and while I was driving home to spend the day with my family, two of my children called me on my cell phone to wish me a happy Father's Day. Yes, you read that correctly; I said two of my children. You see, priests are spiritual fathers, and on this special Sunday, two students that I know very well from their involvement in campus ministry called to let me know that they were thinking of me on Father's Day.

Needless to say, it was a wonderful Father's Day gift; I was truly touched by my students' thoughtfulness. After the call, I thought to myself: *they get it.* They understand the spiritual fatherhood of the priest. I call them "my children" because just as they acknowledged my spiritual fatherhood, I acknowledge that the Lord has entrusted them to my care in a special way. Like all priests, I am called to be a spiritual father, and it brings me a tremendous amount of joy knowing that these two students grasp that reality. This concept is essential for you to understand: you are being called to be a spiritual father. You are not sacrificing fatherhood by becoming a priest; you are embracing it as one of your deepest identities.

People will often ask me, "Father, don't you wish you were married? Don't you wish you had children of your own?" Maybe you have already been asked this question. My response to this question is simple: I am married, and I do have children. Saying that is not wishful or delusional thinking or something I conjure up so that I can "feel good" about myself since I do not have a wife or biological children. Spiritual fatherhood is a profound truth that gives shape to my life. The priest gives himself to the Church as a husband gives himself to his wife, and the priest is called to be a spiritual father to the children that God has entrusted to him.

The great St. Paul wrote about his own spiritual fatherhood to his children in Corinth: "Even if you should have countless guides to Christ, yet you do not have many fathers, for I became your father in Christ Jesus through the gospel" (1 Cor. 4:15). He understood that he was "fathering" his children as he preached the Gospel. And as you read the letters of St. Paul, notice that he had true fatherly concerns— he experienced the anxiety of a father when he worried about his children; he experienced the sorrow and frustration of a father when his children strayed from the path of the Lord; and he experienced the joy and pride of a father when his children made progress in living the Christian life.

If a priest is to live his vocation to the fullest, then grasping this concept of spiritual fatherhood is crucial, just as the seminarian must grasp this concept. Before becoming a priest, you ought to be able to imagine yourself as a good husband and father. If you cannot see yourself as a good husband and father, then you should not believe that you would make a good priest.

Understanding the gift of your masculinity is essential to seeing yourself as a father. God created you as a man, and He is calling you, as a man, to the priesthood. I truly believe that there has been a failure of fatherhood in our society, ultimately because, somewhere along the line, some men stopped being real men. Do not misunderstand me. We all know phenomenal fathers. But we have also witnessed a real failure of fatherhood. Some fathers leave their families, cheat on their wives, abuse their children, or simply do not spend enough time at home with their families. Men are suffering from a deep wound inflicted by this loss of authentic masculinity. Priests can suffer from this wound, as well.

I encourage you to read *Wild at Heart* by John Eldredge, a most insightful book about God's plan for us as men. Eldredge's point is simple, yet profound: we must live out the holy desires that God has placed in our hearts. What are those desires? Eldredge suggests that every man desires a battle to fight, an adventure to live, and a beauty to rescue. We have to be in touch with those desires in our hearts. If a man is struggling with pornography, for example, he needs to examine the authentic, God-given, manly desire hidden beneath the lust. Ultimately, the desire is for union with God. Eldredge rightly contends that when our human fathers fail to initiate us properly into manhood, our power as men comes not from any false outside source, like pornography, but rather from standing confidently in the interior awareness that we are sons of a loving Father. We are initiated into manhood by entering deeply into a relationship with God the Father.

While you are in seminary, reflect on the gift of your manhood. Be open to new insights into authentic Christian manhood. Stand confidently in the awareness that you are a beloved son of the Father. The greatest way to come to a deeper awareness of your sonship is by contemplating the Perfect Man, Jesus Christ. How do you see Jesus as a man? How do you relate to Him as a man? He teaches us how to be true men, how to be sons of the Father, and how to be His friend in friendship's deepest sense.

So, my brother, if you believe you are sacrificing being a father and a husband when you become a priest, you are only partly correct. True, you will not have your own biological children or share marital intimacy with a woman, but you will most certainly exercise your spiritual fatherhood and will be a chaste spouse to the Bride of Christ, the Church.

With prayer for your fatherhood,

Father Najim

Questions for Prayer

Am I deeply aware of my desire to be a father? How can desire help me to be a better priest?

What do I need to do to come to a deeper appreciation for the gift of my masculinity?

The thoughts, feelings, and desires that surfaced as I read this letter:

My prayer:

Balance

*"Do you not know that your body is a
temple of the Holy Spirit within you . . . ?"*
1 Cor. 6:19

My Dear Brother,

Some seminarians experience seminary burnout.
What are the symptoms of seminary burnout? You feel like
your head is spinning and about to explode from the amount
of information you have absorbed during the day. You really
do not feel like going to chapel for Evening Prayer because
you would rather go out for a long walk "to get away from
it all." You are too tired to study, but you have that paper
to write, as well as the rector's conference tonight. The last
thing you feel like doing is going to your field education assignment. You are simply at your wits' end.

Do not worry. These thoughts and feelings are common, and
almost every seminarian experiences them. Take a closer look
at what is happening to you: your body, mind (reason), heart
(affect), and spirit (self-transcendence) are all crying out for
renewal. Listen to them.

When we experience burnout, we are incapable of
being productive in any area of our lives, and we are more
susceptible to temptation. We are too tired to pray, to study,
to socialize, or to exercise. So what do we do? We sleep, we
waste time on mindless activities, or we grab a quick, unhealthy meal that makes us feel even more lethargic.

The key to making sure that you do not burn out is to live a well-balanced life. The seminary is a wonderful place where we are formed in so many valuable ways; however, one area where I believe seminaries can improve is in teaching seminarians the importance of and a plan for *self-leadership*. What do I mean? Simply put, if you cannot lead your own life, then how will you be able to lead others? Leading your own life means having a vision for your life and then living it out. It means having a vision for every area of your life— spiritual, physical, intellectual, social, and emotional. And it means making that vision a reality by your own choices.

If you want to get rid of that lethargic feeling, that haze in your mind, that feeling of burnout, then you must commit to taking care of your whole self. We are temples of the Holy Spirit. God's will is that we be good stewards of ourselves. Unfortunately, too many priests have health issues simply because they have chosen not to take care of themselves. It must not be that way with you. You are responsible for your life, so you must take action to make sure you are healthy in every way. No excuses. After all, if you are not in good health as a priest, how will you have the energy to lead your people closer to the Lord?

Here is what I suggest you do: balance your life so that every day you tend to your whole self: body, mind, heart, and spirit. What does this mean on a practical level? It means that you guard your time of personal prayer; it must be a priority. Your personal prayer is essential, and nothing must interfere with it. You must spend quiet time with the Lord every day so that He can renew your spirit. You must also take care of yourself physically. Are you exercising at least three days a week or more? Are you eating healthy foods? Are you getting enough sleep? If you are not taking care of your body, every other area of your life will be negatively affected. Furthermore, you must nourish your intellectual life. You must carve out time for study but also for reading in other areas that interest you, even if you only have time for short articles from periodicals or the Internet. Just as you guard your prayer, you must also guard your study time. Additionally, make sure that you have a good, healthy social life. Do not be a recluse, but do not spend all of your time in the common room either. Spend quality time with your friends in uplifting conversation and also in meaningful, cultural activities.

Living a balanced life takes initiative on your part. The only one who can take care of yourself is you. What will it take to achieve this balance? It will require saying *yes* and *no*. You have to say *yes* to creating a plan for your life, which means you have to say *no* to those things that stop you from being balanced. You have to say *yes* to prayer, which might mean that you have to say *no* to thirty more minutes of sleep—or you may need to get to bed thirty minutes earlier. You have to say *yes* to your physical health, which means that you have to say *no* to unhealthy foods and to your aversion to physical activity. You have to say *yes* to study, which means that you may have to say *no* to too much time in the common room, in front of the television, or surfing the Web. You have to say *yes* to working on good relationships in your life, which means that you may have to say *no* to your desire to stay alone in your room every night.

When I was in seminary, I did not realize the importance of this balance. Now, as a priest, I recognize that it is one of the most important lessons that I have learned. A book that really helped me to understand this concept of balance is *The 7 Habits of Highly Effective People* by Stephen Covey. I would urge you to read this book and to put into practice the principles that it teaches.

Take care of yourself in every way. The more whole you are in body, mind, heart, and spirit, the holier you will be. Remember, though, the balance is up to you. Do not give into discouragement if you make a resolution to balance your life and to take care of yourself and then fail after one or two days. Keep going. It takes a while to form new habits. One way to make sure that you are committing yourself to a balanced life is by finding someone to keep you accountable. Ask another seminarian to exercise with you, to challenge you in your diet, to check on you to make sure you are praying. I can assure you that if you continually foster balance in your life, you will have more energy and confidence and, ultimately, will not get burned out.

With prayer for balance,

Father Najim

Questions for Prayer

In what area of my life do I need to improve the most (spiritual, intellectual, social, physical)? How can I improve?

What are some practical ways that I can begin to bring more balance to my life?

The thoughts, feelings, and desires that surfaced as I read this letter:

My prayer:

Back to the Place of Encounter

My Dear Brother,

I wrote my first letter to you from a coffee shop in Providence, Rhode Island, a place bustling with activity; my last letter to you is written from a place of silence. This is a little place that I love, a tiny slice of paradise. I am spending a couple days of retreat at St. Edmund's on Enders Island in Mystic, Connecticut. You do not need a boat to get to this 12-acre island. As you turn off the main road, you drive about two miles, watch for the signs, and then pass over a short causeway. Once you cross, straight ahead, you glimpse the tip of the bell tower of a beautiful stone chapel which overlooks the ocean. The water surrounds you here. Upon arrival, you walk down the main pathway, pass the chapel on your left, and beyond the manicured shrubbery set behind a group of trees, you see a white gazebo. As you sit in the rocking chair under the gazebo, you see, almost directly in front of you about thirty yards away, a statue of the Blessed Mother nestled inside a tall blue triangular backdrop. If the statue were back any farther, she would be in the ocean. When you turn slightly to the right and look out, you see a lighthouse in the distance. Sailboats dot the sea. The summer sun beats down today, but the heat is tempered by the ocean breeze. Throughout the day and into the evening, the birds serenade you with their songs. Peace.

I hear the Lord speak to my heart here. He always does. It is difficult *not* to hear Him in a place like this. Being

133

here draws me into silence, into the depths of His love. The sea alone reminds me of Jesus' words, "Put out into deep water" (Lk. 5:4). We can always hear His voice if we learn to be silent and to listen.

Coming away to a place like this, a place that draws us into silence, is not always possible; but on a daily basis, we can enter into silence with the Lord. Every day, we can enter into our hearts, the place of encounter. There, we can enter more deeply into the heart of Christ. We can enter His embrace. We can hear Him speak to us.

I hope these letters have helped you enter more deeply into prayer, into the embrace of Christ. I hope these insights have led you to a deeper understanding of His love for you. I hope the fire of desire to be a good and holy priest has grown stronger in your heart.

My brother, I want you to know that I pray for you daily. You are needed. And you are good. You must receive the truth, in the depth of your heart, that you are a good man. You are a beloved son of the Father. Your weaknesses do not define you; your sonship does. He wants to do great things in and through you. Let Him love you. Every day, let Him speak his love to you.

As I finish this letter, it is nighttime. The moon is shining on the ocean now. The stillness beckons me. I will go and listen. But I already know what He wants me to hear; He tells me time and time again: *My son, I love you. Rest in me.*

What Blessed Columba Marmion, OSB, Can Teach: A Conference for Seminarians

"The priest is the living and transparent image of Christ the priest." So wrote Pope John Paul II in his Post-Synodal Apostolic Exhortation, *Pastores Dabo Vobis*, which focuses on the formation of priests in present-day circumstances. The priest, by virtue of his ordination, is configured to Christ the Priest in a unique way. The man who is ordained a priest receives a sacramental character that conforms him, in his very being, to the Person of Christ, Head and Shepherd of the Church. Thus, the priest is ontologically changed; he truly acts *in persona Christi capitis* (in the Person of Christ as head). He is a priest in his very being, "a priest forever" (Heb. 7:3).

Just because the priest is sacramentally united to Christ, however, does not necessarily mean that the priest always reflects the Person of Christ in his character. As we have recently seen from the sexual abuse crisis, priests often fail to live out their union with Christ in a way that reflects divine charity to God's children. In order for the priest to grow in the grace of his ordination, in order for him to truly make Christ's love present in the world, he must, before all else, be a man of intense prayer.

The priest is the living and transparent image of Christ the Priest. In his priestly life, he must allow himself to be conformed more and more to the Person of Christ. Christ must be his model. Christ must be his all. On September 3, 2000, Pope John Paul II beatified Columba Marmion, along with Pope John XXIII. Columba Marmion was the abbot of the Benedictine Abbey in Maredsous, Belgium. Reading Marmion's spiritual writings was a turning point in my spiritual life. He was a man who was steeped in theological knowledge which penetrated his soul so that these truths became a *lived doctrine.* His whole life as a priest was dedicated to contemplating, and allowing himself to be conformed to, the Person of Christ and His mysteries. Marmion's writings clearly illustrate that he had an intimate love and knowledge of Christ and His Mysteries.

How can Marmion help us to grasp the importance of prayer in the life of the priest? His writings focused on the Person of Christ and the graces that Christ, as man, merited for us. For Marmion, "the priestly life, like the Christian life itself, must be envisaged as dominated by Christ and in constant dependence on His merits, His grace and His activity."[9]

"Nothing is little in the life of Jesus."[10] One of Marmion's central themes was the Incarnation of the Word. When God became man in the Person of Christ He united Himself with every person. Everything changed when the Word became flesh. Marmion contemplated and came to a deep knowledge of the transforming effects of the Incarnation on the human person. He always encouraged his monks to contemplate the Person and work of Christ so that they could marvel at the dignity they possessed in Christ. Now, in Christ, our human nature can be divinized. When we contemplate Christ in His humanity and respond in love, we are conformed more and more to His Person.

Christ lived a real human life. He loved with a human heart. He lived a life of prayer, of chastity, and of obedience to the Father. And because Jesus lived these mysteries as man, He merited for us the grace to live them as well. In other words, we are able to live chaste celibacy because Christ lived it. We are able to pray to the Father because Christ did. We are able to live in obedience to the Father because Christ lived it perfectly. Christ, as man, merited for us the grace to live His mysteries. But only by prayerfully contemplating His Person and actions are we conformed to Him.

When we contemplate a particular mystery in the life of Christ, *we receive the particular grace that Christ merited for us in that mystery.* For example, when we contemplate Christ in Gethsemane, we are conformed more deeply to His filial obedience, to His surrender to the Father's will. The priest needs to have a deep prayer life so that his whole person can be conformed to the Person of Christ. The mind of the priest is to be conformed to the mind of Christ; the heart of the priest is to be conformed to the heart of Christ, and the passions of the priest are to be conformed to the passions of Christ.

The priest is called to make divine charity present in the world through his ministry. But loving with the heart of Christ is impossible if the priest is not seeking union with Christ. So, what should be at the heart of the priest's life of prayer? Above all else, the priest should have within himself *a deep desire to be in union with Christ*. And this desire for union with Christ ought to be expressed in his prayer. Priests are called to continue the ministry of Christ; therefore, they must always live in union with Him so that their ministry will be fruitful. Prayer is the fuel that sustains the priest in his pastoral charity. Without prayer, the ministry of the priest simply becomes activism. To prevent such a reduction of life from happening to the priest, the Church *binds* him to prayer.

1. On the day of your diaconate ordination, in addition to promises of celibacy and obedience, you will promise to pray faithfully the Liturgy of the Hours for the Church and the world. This is not an option. The priest is called to pray the Divine Office *for the Church*. Many priests have abandoned the breviary. Such an unfortunate reality is difficult to understand because those priests promised to pray it. Recently, I heard about a priest who is less then five years ordained. He said that he has stopped praying the breviary because "it doesn't do anything" for him. The purpose of the breviary is not primarily to do something for

the priest (although it does). The priest is asked to pray it for the Church and for the world. The Church is depending on priests to pray the Divine Office—*for the people!*

As ordained priests, we cannot just haphazardly put aside the breviary. Is it difficult sometimes? Yes. Does it become rote at times? Certainly. Does it feel like a burden some days? Absolutely. But praying the Office is for the people. I always try to remind myself that my prayer is for the people. The words of the Psalms so often echo the cries of the people ("My God, my God, why have you abandoned me?" Psalm 22:2). The Liturgy of the Hours keeps us rooted. It refocuses us every day on the purpose of our lives: to love, to serve, and to pray for God's people. And it deepens our conformity with Christ. How? *Because the Psalms that we pray are the same Psalms that came from the heart and lips of Christ.* Christ prayed the same Psalms that we are praying.

2. Priests are ordained to offer the sacrifice of the Mass. The identity of the priest is seen most profoundly when he offers the Mass. He stands at the altar offering the same sacrifice Christ offered on Calvary. The priest lends his humanity to Christ so that Christ can be made present in the Eucharist. If the prayer life of the priest is meant to deepen his conformity with Jesus Christ, then offering the Mass faithfully and reverently is

the greatest way the priest can be conformed to Christ.

The deepest union between the priest and Christ occurs when the priest celebrates Mass worthily. When the priest consecrates the Eucharist, he ought to allow himself to be taken up into the very mystery of Christ, into the very heart of Christ. The faithful, daily celebration of Holy Mass is indispensable for the prayer life of the priest because the culmination of Christ's life was His sacrificial act of obedience to the Father on the cross. The sacrifice on Calvary is re-presented in the sacrifice of the Mass. When the priest enters mindfully into the celebration of Holy Mass, he is more deeply conformed to the Mysteries he is celebrating, namely, the Passion, Death, and Resurrection of Christ. Marmion puts it this way, "Do we not say 'Holy Mass, Holy Communion'? And why? Because these actions put us in the *immediate contact with the source of all sanctity*."[11]

3. The habit of prayerful meditation is vital for the life of a priest. If we understand Marmion's Christology, we see that meditation conforms us more deeply to Jesus and to the particular mystery we are contemplating. How can the priest impart knowledge of Christ to the people if the priest is not taking time to know Christ himself? How can the priest tell his people to love Christ if he is not taking the time to love Christ himself? Since

140

the Blessed Sacrament ought to be at the center of the priest's life, I find that meditation before the Blessed Sacrament is particularly fruitful. In the midst of the diocesan priest's extremely busy life, setting aside time for silent meditation is important.

Here, I might also add the importance of spiritual reading. Spiritual reading can inspire within us certain affections for Christ. If we are finding meditation difficult or dry, spiritual reading can be a great help. Contemplating Christ in the Gospels is particularly important, not only for the spiritual life of the priest but also for his preaching.

4. Devotion to the Blessed Virgin is indispensable for the priest. If the priest is called to live in union with Christ and to try to remain recollect in the midst of the world, then he must rely on the help of Our Lady. She, more than anyone, was conformed to the Person of Christ and His mysteries. The life of the priest will be fruitful if he lives in Mary. In her, he will be able to love Christ more deeply. The priest should stay close to Mary always, for just as she carried Christ in her womb and held Him in her arms, so the priest holds Christ daily in his hands when he says "this is my body ... this is my blood" (Mt. 26:26, 28). If the priest lives in Mary, he will be conformed more deeply to Christ because he will begin to

see with her eyes and love with her heart. The rosary is a great help in contemplating Christ in His mysteries with the heart of Mary.

5. I am a sinner. I fall short of the ideals for which we should be striving as priests. My prayer life is imperfect. I do not always spend as much time in prayer as I should. Many days, I fail to make the charity of Christ present to others. I thank the Father for the gift of Reconciliation. The priest must make Confession a central component in his spiritual life. The priest must go to Confession regularly because there he receives the grace to grow in holiness. If he is to be a minister of God's mercy, he must frequently receive it. If he is to be a good confessor, he must be a good penitent. Pope John Paul II states in *Pastores Dabo Vobis*, "'If a priest were no longer to go to confession or properly confess his sins, his priestly being and his priestly action would feel its effects very soon, and this would also be noticed by the community of which he was the pastor'" (PDV, 26). If the priest fosters a love for Confession, his whole being will be more and more conformed to the Person of Christ.

Priests are called to be men passionately in love with Jesus Christ. Our beloved late Holy Father, Pope John Paul II, called the Church to a *new evangelization*, and he stated that priests are to be the first apostles of the *new evangelization*. Priests are called to make Christ known and loved.

But they can make Christ known and loved only if they are striving to know and love Him more deeply. Christians are called to surrender their lives to Christ, but the people need someone to teach them how to surrender. If a priest has not totally surrendered his life to Christ, then he cannot expect that his people will. And even if the priest is not completely surrendered to Christ, he must at least pray for *the desire to desire* to surrender to Christ. Prayer must be at the heart of the life of every priest. He cannot live without it. It must be the air he breathes. My brothers, your ministry as priests will not be fruitful if you do not pray. The Church and the world need passionate, holy priests. The people desire holy priests. Priests sell their people short if they do not pray.

I encourage you to read Blessed Columba Marmion. You will find in him a treasure of wisdom that will greatly affect your spiritual life. I also ask you to pray for me. I am imperfect, but I pray for the grace to be a holy priest. My prayer for you is that you will find within yourself a desire to be in intimate union with Christ. I pray that you find within yourself a desire to surrender to Christ. I pray that you will be holy priests; for if you are holy priests, your people will be holy; and if the people are holy, the world will be transformed. Priests are the first apostles of the *new evangelization*. I pray that, through prayer, our hearts will burn with the same fire of the first apostles to make Christ known and loved in the world.

Notes

1   Joseph Ratzinger, *Called to Communion* (San Francisco: Ignatius Press, 1996), 128.

2   Dynamics of prayer taught by The Institute for Priestly Formation in Omaha, Nebraska (Acknowledge, Relate, Receive, Respond).

3   St. Josemaría Escrivá, *The Way, Furrow, The Forge* (Manila: Sinag-Tala Publishers, 1994), 15, #64.

4   Father Timothy Gallagher, *The Discernment of Spirits* (New York: The Crossroad Publishing Company, 2005), 49-50, 61.

5   These points are taken almost verbatim from Timothy Gallagher, OMV, *The Examen Prayer: Ignatian Wisdom for Our Lives Today* (New York: The Crossroad Publishing Company, 2006), 25.

6   Benedict J. Groeschel, CFR, and Terrence L. Weber, *Thy Will Be Done: A Spiritual Portrait of Terence Cardinal Cooke* (New York: Alba House, 1990), 210.

7   St. Josemaría Escrivá, *The Way, Furrow, The Forge* (Manila: Sinag Tala Publishers, 1994), 177, #709.

8   St. Augustine, *Commentary on the Psalms Ps. 60, 2-3: CCL 39, 766.*

9   Columba Marmion, *Christ, the Ideal of the Priest* (St. Louis: B. Herder Book Co., 1952), 11.

10   Columba Marmion, *Christ in His Mysteries* (St. Louis: B. Herder Book Co., 1939), 7.

11   Columba Marmion, *Christ, the Ideal of the Priest*, 179.